SEP 1 0 2015

Decorate your
SHOES

Create Original FOOTWEAR

Located in Paducah, Kentucky, the American Quilter's Society (AQS) is dedicated to promoting the accomplishments of today's quilters. Through its publications and events, AQS strives to honor today's quiltmakers and their work and to inspire future creativity and innovation in quiltmaking.

EXECUTIVE BOOK EDITOR: ANDI MILAM REYNOLDS
COPY EDITOR: CHRYSTAL ABHALTER
GRAPHIC DESIGN: MELISSA POTTERBAUM
COVER DESIGN: MICHAEL BUCKINGHAM
PHOTOGRAPHY: CHARLES R. LYNCH
ADDITIONAL PHOTOGRAPHY: ANNEMART BERENDSE

Special thanks to shoe model: Marcelle Cashon

American Quilter's Society
P. O. Box 3290 • Paducah, KY 42002-3290
www.AmericanQuilter.com

ATTENTION PHOTOCOPYING SERVICE: Please note the following —Publisher and author give permission to print pages 71-77 for personal use only.

Additional copies of this book may be ordered from the American Quilter's Society, PO Box 3290, Paducah, KY 42002-3290, or online at www.AmericanQuilter.com.

LIBRARY OF CONGRESS CATALOGING-IN-PUBLICATION DATA

Berendse, Annemart.
  Decorate your shoes! : create one-of-a-kind footwear / by Annemart Berendse.
     pages cm
  Summary: "Author provides 11 projects for seven shoe types and explains how to mark on leather, vinyl, and canvas. Embellish and decorate shoes with fabric markers and paints"--Provided by publisher.
  ISBN 978-1-60460-031-5
  1. Painting--Technique. 2. Felt marker decoration--Technique. 3. Decoration and ornament--Themes, motives. 4. Shoes. I. Title.
  TT385.B46 2012
  745.7'23--dc23
                    2012005038

Dedication

This book is dedicated to all the quilters who
dare to do something different,
dare to be creative, and
dare to have fun.

As Katherine Hepburn said,
"If you obey all the rules, you miss all the fun."

Acknowledgments

This book has been a joy to write and would have never seen the world without the contribution and support of so many others.

First and foremost I would like to thank Gloria Bolden and Meredith Schroeder from the American Quilter's Society. I met them in Paducah during the 2011 AQS quilt show. They saw my shoes and asked me to design a pair of quilt shoes on the spot and to send in a book proposal. See here the result! If you are thinking about a book, submit a book proposal. Book proposals are welcome at AQS; check www.americanquilter.com.

I would also like to thank JoAnne Louis from www.paperpieces.com and www.feetofcreativity.com. She was so enthusiastic about my shoes that she introduced me to Gloria from AQS. And then she said I owed her nothing. Sure! Welcome in the new adventure!

Like making a quilt, starting a book is great; finishing it can sometimes be a more difficult phase. The support of my quilt mates—Agnes, Marianne, Debby, Karin, and Ted—was very important, especially in the end. Your enthusiasm, great remarks, and our quilting time filled with joy and laughter are very precious to me.

My mother-in-law, who taught me the first steps in quilting, is now bragging about my quilting. I hope I do her proud.

My spouse and our cat, Splinter, support me in more ways than I could imagine, far above and beyond their call of duty. I think I'll keep them.

But most of all I would like to thank all of the quilters in Paducah who were so enthusiastic about my shoes—and all of the great people I met who told me they would like to read how to make them. Thanks to your inspiring reactions, here's the book.

Enjoy and have fun!

Table of Contents

Introduction

The inspiration for my quilt shoes came when I was packing for a big quilt show. I would be at the show for a few days and on my packing list stood, right below the credit card, comfortable shoes. And then I looked at all the shoes I had. Most of them were suitable for an office environment and fine dining, and only two pairs were the ones I could walk in for ages. One pair had open toes. I don't know whether you have ever been to a big quilt show, but open toe is a no-go area unless you particularly like blue toenails! (I advise nail polish for that.)

And there they were. The white leather clogs; I could walk in them forever. But I did not wear them, as they were white. Very white. And I wanted fun shoes, because quilting is fun for me, and going to a show is the ultimate fun. I had a few days before I would be leaving for the US. And then I got it. I would decorate them into fun shoes for show myself! I grabbed my permanent markers and drew a patchwork pattern on them. Done! Now my suitcase was packed to leave.

During my flight I thought about some more designs I could try and was getting more enthusiastic about the idea to wear my own designed shoes.

In Paducah at the AQS quilt show I was not prepared for what happened! People kept stopping me to look at my shoes, asking to hold them next to my head for a photograph. Imagine that, shoes by my head after walking 3 full days in them!

Sweet people, enthusiastic people, fun people—all of them just coming up and asking. Many of them asked for a book, a pattern, ideas. Some ladies even kept talking to me for 45 minutes, just to know all about it! I met the dearest ladies because of my decorated shoes. They all inspired me to write this book.

This book is not about the finest appliqué, how to get more stitches in an inch, or what you absolutely must and must not do to be that blue ribbon, multi-award-winning quilter. This book is for every quilter who wants to start a fun project; reuse those comfortable once-white shoes; or needs a great project for her guild, quilt bee, or retreat. All of the projects are designed for people who do not have experience decorating shoes. There are simple and more advanced projects; projects for leather, canvas, and vinyl shoes; projects created with paint, and projects made with markers.

When you begin, starting with canvas shoes and simple fabric markers is a great choice. Once you have more experience, leather paint on leather shoes is a good option for a more durable result. Although most projects can be done on all types of shoes, Ribbon City is advised to be executed only on canvas.

Just have fun, and I hope you use this book as an example for your own creativity. As Charlotte Angotti told me during a quilt class:

Like the cab driver in Boston who was sitting next to three other cars in front of a traffic light when only two lanes were available: "The lines are only a suggestion."

Have fun making and wearing your decorated, one-of-a-kind shoes!

General Instructions

Choosing Shoes

Before decorating your shoes, you first have to check the material they are made of. Then think, what are you going to use your shoes for? If it's just for a few days, you don't want to spend too much on your shoes, so shop accordingly. And how will they be used/abused? Will they get wet?

Some shoe materials offer several decoration options, some hardly any. Leather and canvas shoes are preferred when decorating shoes; synthetic shoes of all kinds offer different obstacles that might or might not be overcome. It does not matter whether the shoes are new or old. As long as they are clean and sound and preferably white, you can decorate them as the material dictates.

Material	Pros	Cons
Canvas (natural materials) (Like Toms®, Keds®, Converse®)	• Durable result • Decorate with beads and ribbons more easily • Low cost option • Light weight for traveling	• Rubber soles and front have less durability for decoration • Not suitable for all weather conditions • Less foot support than vinyl or leather, so less suitable for pounding the pavement
Rubber or vinyl (Like Crocs™, Nomad®, parts of running shoes)	• Quick result because of less preparation • Relatively low cost • Suitable for all weather conditions	• Color only with permanent markers • Color will probably fade • Color might smear, bleed, or shed • Less ventilation than canvas or leather
Manmade leather (Check the inside or sole of the shoe for this word; manmade leather is not the same as vinyl)	• Durable result • Stable and smooth surface	• Higher cost option • Material can differ among manufacturers; test-driving necessary
Leather	• Durable result • More foot support and foot comfort • Suitable for all weather conditions • Stable and smooth surface	• Relatively more expensive

Each material needs a specific treatment. However, they all need:

- *Preparing: In this stage the shoe is cleaned and primed for decorating.*
- *Decorating: Specific paint or markers are used to bring out the design.*
- *Finishing: A finish is applied to the paint to secure the design and protect the shoes against dirt, grease, and all the kicks they will have to endure.*

Whatever you choose, get creative, have fun, and enjoy!

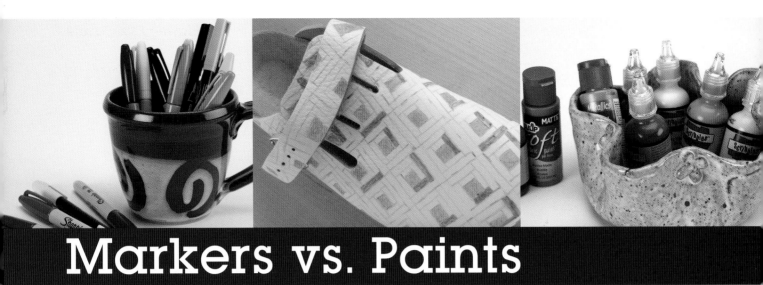

Markers vs. Paints

Fabric Markers

Fabric markers can be found for a few dollars for a set of 12 at your local dollar store or for about $3 per single professional textile marker in an art shop. Differences are found in the amount of colors offered, the quality of the pen and the ink/paint, and the different choices in tips. A starter set of 8 to 12 colors, including black, is great to begin with. Beginning is easy, because fabric markers can be used layered, and mistakes made with lighter colors are easily disguised. Prepare your shoes, get your markers, and just get started!

At a more advanced level, look for fabric markers with a wider range of tips. A chisel tip is your first choice for filling larger surfaces, a fine point is great for drawing details, and a brush tip is excellent for drawing with a fluid stroke.

Besides the choice in tips, most professional textile markers contain ink or paint that has more depth and is wetter, so you can create blended effects and mix colors more easily. Added to the difference in quality, the choice in colors and the options that different tips offer, these professional markers make the investment worthwhile when progressing in shoe decoration.

How to start with fabric markers?
Fabric markers are as simple as working with crayons on a coloring picture. When you have drawn the design on the shoe with pencil, you can start filling in. As the marker is a bit opaque, start with a light color.

Mixing colors is not an option for the lower priced brands, but the higher range markers are suitable for blending by laying one layer over another.

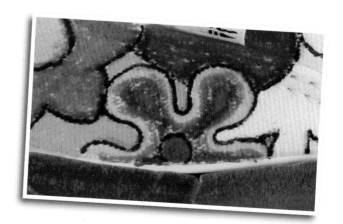

With fabric markers the color is applied in lines. That gives you the opportunity to create color effects like a small rainbow within a flower.

On larger surfaces, fabric markers usually give a bit of an uneven result. However, at a distance, and usually that would be 5 feet from the eyes to the floor, it does not show.

What if you make a mistake?

Fabric markers are usually based on acrylic paint. That means cotton swabs, water, and a little soap may save the day if you slipped with your marker minutes ago. Be careful not to spill water on the places that you want to keep, and let the spot you work on dry before putting on another layer of paint.

If you notice later the color is in a wrong spot, your cotton swab, water, and soap might still save you with pastels, but the brighter colors will have been absorbed fully into the shoe material. Putting a darker color on over a mistake is a second best option.

Your last option: Decide that the slip-up is part of your design and you wanted it to be that way. You reform the big blob into a flower, or you put an embellishment like a button or a ribbon on it. At 5 feet of distance, a lot can be hidden.

What to buy?

For beginners a basic set of fabric markers from Edding®, a German brand; Stained! by Sharpie™; or Tulip® Fabric Markers™ fine tip are a great investment. These all have a color collection of 8 to 20 markers for a reasonable price. Very fine black contour lines are made with an ultrafine or fine permanent marker, such as a Sharpie® or a Bic®. If you wish to develop further or already know that you will need more colors and more artistic options than a starter set can offer you, FabricMate™, Rayher®, and Marabu offer a great range of colors and tips.

Permanent Markers

> **Note:** *Working with general permanent markers on canvas shoes might seem attractive but may result in disappointment. Permanent markers on fabric may bleed when wet, and the design might get a yellow halo around it. With special fabric markers you avoid that risk.*

The Sharpie website (www.sharpie.com) states that a marker is defined as waterproof if the writing is still legible after it comes in contact with water. That definition implies that it doesn't mean the ink will stay on forever. However, with the right preparation, you will have a lot of fun for a longer time with this simple and low-cost option. Just do not expect to have a design for a lifetime and be aware of shedding and smearing.

The number of colors available is an asset, as mixing colors is not an option. Buy a set with fine tips that has all the colors you would like to use on your shoe. Because in all designs black is a must, an extra set of black fine points for the outer contrast line is advised. If you are planning on coloring large surfaces and/or adding many very fine details, consider the purchase of a set of chisel tip markers and a set of markers with an ultrafine tip.

When working with permanent markers, wear clothes that have seen their best part in life a long time ago. Permanent marker ink is not removed easily. Ink on your hands is best removed with an antibacterial hand sanitizer with alcohol.

Markers vs. Paints

How to start with permanent markers?

Permanent markers are just like fabric markers: just fill out the design and enjoy! Thin layers do the trick. Just keep in mind that when an area of just-colored ink is not completely dry, it might bleed or mix with the color you are trying to put next to it. Therefore, as with fabric markers, start with light colors and keep on going darker, and let the ink dry before applying a color next to it. In the designs in this book, you will always end with a black marker for the contour lines. This will fix any small mistake or uneven line between patches.

With permanent markers it is possible to create textures by the way you use the marker.

Take a marker with a fine tip, and of a light color, to make a plain color with straight lines for a lined background.

 Take a marker of a light color, use the fine or chisel tip, and make a plain color by circling the tip around for a cloudy background.

When the background is dry, you can put on details with a fine or ultrafine permanent marker. Be sure to work with dark on light.

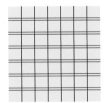 

Working with light on dark will not work and the tip of your light marker might absorb the dark color.

If you would like to work with light details on a dark background, plan your design upfront.

First, draw the details with pencil on the patch where you want to work (figure 1). Then start with the light color on the details you want to color (figure 2). Then color the background (figure 3). All details are outlined in black to create sharp edges and contrast. Here stars are used, but maybe flowers or roses are more your style.

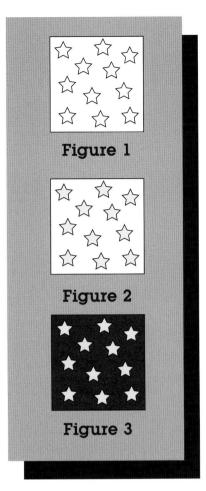

Figure 1

Figure 2

Figure 3

What if you make a mistake?

It may happen that you color on the wrong spot, or the cat jumped on your lap, causing you to slip with your marker across the shoe. Don't panic. That's where cotton swabs and alcohol come in. Take a cotton swab, dip it in the alcohol and squeeze it a bit, so it's moist, not wet. Then go over the area with the unwanted color with the cotton swab and carefully wet the ink with the alcohol. The alcohol will dilute the ink, whilst the cotton swab absorbs the color. If the area gets very wet, use a dry cotton swab. Each time use a new cotton swab to prevent shedding from the cotton swab to the shoe. The ink might not come off completely, especially not with darker colors, but enough to cover it up with a new color layer.

12

What to buy?

Permanent markers are widely available and nowadays loads of colors are offered. I prefer Sharpies because of their wide color range. The reds and oranges tend to fade more than the other colors. CD/DVD-markers and permanent markers for transparencies are available in a very limited color range, but may hold better. For reds and oranges I use Staedtler® Lumocolor®, but you may try any regular CD/DVD-marker. Whatever you buy, don't spend too much on it. A project on rubber and vinyl shoes is just for fun and for the short term!

Fabric Paint

If you have a steady hand, are an experienced painter, or want to experiment with mixing colors, fabric paint is another option. Fabric paint is available in monochromatic colors (unicolors, or unis, in some circles), and be certain to check out the metallic, glitter, and pearl varieties. With fabric markers it is simple to draw the design on the shoe and just starting filling in with the colors you have. With fabric paint you can experiment with a cloudy background brought on with cotton wool or a sponge, try different tones and hues, and even add transparency in your work.

How to start with fabric paint?

Working with paint gives you loads of opportunities and therefore requires more preparation when thinking about your design and which colors to use. Being able to create new colors is one of the biggest advantages to fabric paint. When you have mixed a color, you might not be able to recreate it for your second shoe. Mix enough of the color at once for both shoes so there will be no color difference. Before you start coloring, have both shoes ready with the pencil design drawn on both. Then you can apply the mixed color for both shoes at once.

It is important to work in several thin layers instead of one single thick layer to create a deeper color and better adherence. At the same time you prevent dripping and smearing.

What if you make a mistake?

If your hand tried a move on its own and the fabric paint is not on the spot where you wanted it, use a cotton swab and dip it in water. Squeeze it so it's moist (not wet), and remove the paint as much as you can. Use a new cotton swab each time to prevent shedding. When ready, work on another area until the treated area has dried.

Other solution: use an opaque color on the area where your mistake occurred. As if nothing happened! And it's not a mistake—it's your artistic license.

What to buy?

For brands I prefer Talens textile paint (Dutch brand, available at http://iartsupplies.co.uk/, English website) because of their wide range of opaque and transparent uni (monochromatic) colors and the quality of the paint, and Textile Colors and Lumiere from Jacquard, especially for the wide range of metallics and pearl paint. Lumiere is widely available, and is also applicable to (manmade) leather. If you plan on working both on fabric and (manmade) leather shoes, Lumiere is a great choice.

Leather Paint

Working with leather paint is suitable for beginners as well as for the more advanced. Where beginners might start with larger areas, those who have more experience might work in finer detail or freehand.

How to start with leather paint?
Most important is to work in thin layers and to work with a soft brush. The soft brush prevents brush marks showing on your paintwork, and the thin layers dry faster and deepen your chosen color. The thin layers will also hold better in the long term. Do not hurry, just keep on going, layer by layer. Before putting on another layer, wait at least 15 minutes; then you are sure a thin layer has dried. If you work on wet paint or the layer below is too thick, the new layer will brush away the layer underneath leaving a smudgy and clotted area. If that happens, moisten a cotton swab and clean the area. Let it dry and start all over with patience and thin layers.

Mixing colors creates more colors than you might think of. Mix small amounts of a dark color in a light color to find the color you want. Be sure to add the darker color to a lighter color, and not the other way around. Darkening a color is easier than lightening a black to a gray. Use a saucer or a plate to mix on and compare different mixed colors on a piece of paper.

There are two main brands of leather paint—Angelus® and Jacquard. With Angelus paint there is the option

to dilute your color with the color neutral. It makes the color more transparent. A tiny spot of green in neutral gives a beautiful transparent mint green. Be sure to add the color to the neutral paint, and not the other way around. Jacquard offers the same option with Neopaque Colorless Extender.

Both paints are acrylic paints and water-based. Diluting with water creates a watercolor paint. Don't add more than 25 percent water; otherwise, your paint will be more like water and might run where you don't want it to.

When you mix a color that you would like to use on both shoes, mix it for both shoes at once and have both shoes ready, pattern drawn on and all; you will never be able to create exactly the same color again. Be aware that Angelus metallic paints require a background color. This table will help you determine which ground color is for which metallic paint.

Angelus Color	Background Color
Gold	Yellow
Silver, Pewter	Gray
Copper, Bronze	Brown

For example, when working with Angelus gold, first paint the area yellow with a few thin layers. Then put a few layers of gold on.

What if you make a mistake?

If your hand tried a move on its own and the fabric paint is not on the spot where you wanted it, use a cotton swab and dip it in water. Squeeze it so it's moist (not wet), and remove the paint as much as you can. Use a new cotton swab each time to prevent shedding. When ready, work on another area until the treated area has dried.

If your stain is a bit older, use a tiny bit of acetone on your cotton swab. That will also take away the dried layer underneath.

Final solution: Use an opaque color on the area where your mistake occurred. It will be as if nothing happened!

What to buy?

Jacquard Lumiere and Neopaque offer a great range of metallics and a smaller range of uni (monochromatic) colors. The Jacquard colors are in general shiny and searching for attention. Angelus leather paint offers a very wide range of uni colors and neons and a smaller range of metallics. Angelus colors tend to be more matte.

It depends on the material of the shoe, the purpose of the shoe, and the colors I choose which range I'm going for. For everyday leather office shoes, I usually focus on uni colors with a metallic accent and choose from the wide range of Angelus leather paints. Always, when I have to deal with manmade leather shoes for a pair of party shoes or some eccentric show-offs, I will choose Jacquard. Each has its advantages.

Jacquard offers a great starter set with the Lumiere & Neopaque paints with nine colors. This is enough for three pairs of shoes. Angelus offers a starter set with 11 one-ounce bottles including gold and a bottle of neutral, enough to create 10 pairs of shoes.

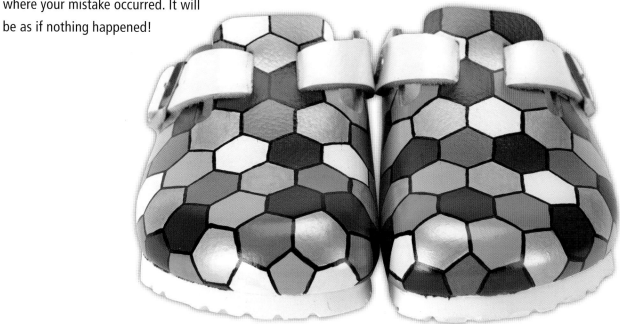

Preparing, Decorating, and Finishing

Canvas Shoes

Canvas shoes are a great option for your first decorated pair, or an extra pair to add to your new shoe collection. Just get crazy and try a new design or a new technique with markers or with textile paint.

When you are looking for the right shoes, keep in mind that white gives the best color effect as it doesn't influence the marker or paint colors, and choose a shoe with as little rubber as possible. Rubber is not as easy to decorate as canvas. Check for canvas made from natural fibers, as these absorb the paint better than synthetic fibers.

> *Preparing canvas shoes*
> **Necessary items:**
> • **Washing machine**
> • **Masking tape**

Whether you use new shoes or want to decorate your old ones you've used for years, first wash them. New canvas shoes might be prepared with an extra finish layer to resist staining and the paint may not attach to the material. Your old shoes carry the result of using them and every bit of grease or dirt on them prevents the paint from adhering to the fabric.

Just put them for a short cycle in the washing machine with a little normal commercial detergent on a low temperature and end with a slow spin. Hang them on a clothesline to air dry. Use the dryer at your own risk. The material in the shoe might shrink due to the heat and your shoe might end up a few sizes smaller.

Apply masking tape to the areas you want to prevent from coloring, such as soles and rubber toe tops, and remove the laces.

Decorating canvas shoes

To start decorating your canvas shoes, you will need the following basic supplies:

* Fabric markers or fabric paint
* A blow dryer or small iron system (like the quilt irons from Clover or Prym-Dritz)
* A black ultrafine permanent marker
* Cotton swabs
* Advised: water repellent spray

If you choose to work with fabric paint, you will also need:

- Two soft brushes: a small straight-edge brush for larger areas and a small round brush for details, lines, and correcting mistakes.
- Two jars of plain water, one for cleaning your brushes, one for correcting mistakes. Replace the last one every time it is used. Replace the first one regularly.

To choose what to use, markers or paint, it depends on how much money you want to spend and how much experience you have working with paint.

Finishing canvas shoes

Most brands of fabric paint and fabric markers have to be set by heat. After setting the paint, the shoes can be washed and used outside without the risk of finding the paint on your socks and the design gone. Finishing is done by ironing with a small iron on the backside of the material. A small iron like the Clover craft mini iron or the Prym-Dritz mini steam iron are helpful.

Check whether the backside of the material does not have a rubber coating; otherwise, your precious iron will be full of melted rubber. When in doubt, use a pressing sheet between the iron and the material to prevent tacking. If you have some time to spare, use a hair dryer, put it on high, and just blow away at a 6″ distance. Moving slowly, blow dry every part of the shoe and don't stay at one spot for more than 10 seconds to prevent overheating. Fifteen minutes for one shoe will do the trick. Because of the chances of shrinking, the option of using the dryer is at your own risk.

Optional is the treatment of your shoes with water repellent spray. It protects your feet from getting wet and your design from bleeding, if in the ironing process you missed a spot.

Rubber and Vinyl Shoes

Rubber and vinyl shoes (including rubber toes and soles on canvas shoes) can only be decorated with permanent markers. Because the ink of the markers is not absorbed by the material, the ink is vulnerable and will fade very easily and might even bleed when wet. For the latter, keep your decoration away from the side of the shoe so you will not end up with blue feet or rainbow-colored socks. Decorating this kind of shoe is a fun project for the reuse of your long forgotten light Crocs or those flip-flops that are just too white. Do not expect the design to hold for the years to come! To upgrade these shoes, don't forget embellishments. The material has no effect on that.

> **Preparing rubber and vinyl shoes**
> **Necessary items:**
> - **Soft cloth**
> - **Water and soap**
> - **Kitchen towels**
> - **Alcohol (70-95%)**
> - **Cotton wool**
> - **600 grit or superfine sandpaper**
> - **Masking tape**

For preparation of your rubber or vinyl shoes, first clean them with soap to wash a possible protective layer off. Moisten your soft cloth, apply a little soap, and wring it until damp, definitely not wet. Then carefully clean the outside of the shoe with the cloth. Wipe the shoe dry with kitchen towels.

To give the permanent marker ink a better surface to hold onto, treat the parts you want to decorate with superfine sandpaper. I use 600 grit. The effect of the sanding is not visible, and it gives the ink some grip.

The next step is cleaning with alcohol. As alcohol is very flammable, stay away from fire and hot objects.

If you are working in a small area, make sure there is enough ventilation. When working with chemicals, keep children and pets out of the way. Take a soft cloth or cotton wool, wet it with alcohol, and clean the outside of your shoe with it. The alcohol will evaporate very quickly.

Make sure the alcohol is evaporated fully before starting with permanent markers. The ink of permanent markers is based on alcohol, and a mere drop of alcohol will dilute the ink and make it bleed.

Apply masking tape to the areas you want to prevent from coloring, such as soles and rubber toe tops.

Decorating rubber and vinyl shoes
Tools and supplies for working with permanent markers on rubber or vinyl:
- Permanent markers, including black
- Alcohol (70-95%)
- Cotton swabs
- Anti-bacterial hand sanitizer (with alcohol)

Finishing rubber and vinyl shoes
Patience is the only thing you need when working with permanent markers. If you use a chisel tip marker, or put several layers of ink on each other, drying may take several days. Be careful to let your shoes dry totally free of touching anything so smearing and shedding is prevented. Your shoes are dry when they do not feel sticky anymore when you touch them. Hair dryers or heating will not help; it's not about drying the ink, it's about hardening it. And that means patience.

When dry, heat and wetness may cause shedding, so cover them carefully and separately when packing for the quilt show.

Leather and Manmade Leather Shoes

Leather and manmade leather shoes can be decorated with permanent markers for a quick result. Look at pages 11-12 on how to decorate rubber and vinyl shoes with permanent markers if you want a quick result.

A more durable option that's also applicable to manmade leather shoes is painting them with paint manufactured for this purpose. If you want to use manmade leather, be certain that it's stated on the shoe. Vinyl shoes that appear to be leather are absolutely not suitable for decorating with paint.

Although manmade leather and leather are prepared the same way, be aware that manmade leather can only be painted with one brand of paint: Jacquard, paint types Lumiere and Neopaque. Leather can be painted with either Jacquard Lumiere and Neopaque, or Angelus leather paint. Each has a similar preparation, but a different finishing. Mixing the two brands is not advised, as the Lumiere demands a shoe with wax finishing, while the Angelus demands an acrylic-coated shoe.

Preparing manmade and natural leather shoes

For working with permanent markers on (manmade) leather shoes, apply the same preparation, materials for decoration, and finishing as with rubber and vinyl shoes. With a correct preparation a possible stain protective layer will be removed, but the wax and the color stays on. If you choose this option, go for white shoes. A darker color may affect the perceived color of your permanent markers. On leather shoes, permanent markers bond better, although the colors might fade in time. If at a later stage you decide to color your leather shoes with paint, follow the preparation procedure as for painting leather shoes.

> ### Preparing (manmade) leather shoes for working with paint, you will need the following:
> - Acetone (at your local hardware store)
> - Lots of cotton wool
> - Household gloves
> - Protective mask
> - Cotton swabs for the tiny edges
> - Masking tape

To prepare leather or manmade leather shoes for paint, I use acetone. Although Jacquard advises the use of alcohol for preparation of leather shoes, I think cleaning with acetone gives a steadier base. For preparing for Angelus paint, Angelus advises their special Preparer-Deglazer, but as that is not available to the European market, I replaced it with acetone, and it works fine.

Do not use nail polish remover based on acetone, as it contains a fatty conditioner that will prevent the paint from attaching to the shoe and is far more expensive.

As acetone is highly flammable and creates toxic fumes, be certain to wear a mask and have enough ventilation or work outside. Do not smoke and stay away from fire and hot objects. Wear household gloves to protect your hands and nails from dehydration. Keep children and pets away.

Wet the cotton wool with the acetone. Give the area on the shoe you want to work on a good rub. With the acetone you are removing all chemicals and a part of the color. It might take 15 minutes before you have all chemicals and color removed. The result of the treatment with acetone will differ according to the shoe. A high quality leather shoe might feel a bit rough, but hardly any change is visible. A shoe from manmade leather, on the other hand, may be stripped bare of its paint, look grayish, and leave you with loads of dirty cotton wool full of sticky paint.

This is the base you are working on. Be careful to keep this base as clean as possible. Any grease or dirt may prevent the paint from adhering to your shoe. So, no chocolate or cookies while painting! Because you have treated the upper completely with acetone, the protecting layer is gone. That means that the whole surface needs to be painted. In patterns where areas are left white, for leather that means decorating with white leather paint.

Apply masking tape to the areas you want to prevent from coloring, such as soles and rubber toe tops.

Decorating manmade and natural leather shoes with paint

To start decorating your manmade leather or natural leather shoes, you will need the following basic supplies:

- Jacquard Lumiere and Neopaque paint for manmade leather and leather shoes or Angelus leather paint for leather shoes. Do not mix both brands, especially not for manmade leather.

- A toothpick to draw small lines, or if you do not trust your nerves, an ultrafine permanent marker in black.

- Soft brushes, a small straight-edge ruler for lining large areas, a fan brush for filling large areas, and a tiny round one for details.

- 2 jars of plain water, 1 for cleaning your brushes, 1 for correcting mistakes. Replace the last one every time it is used. Replace the first one regularly.

- Cotton swabs.

Finishing leather and manmade leather shoes

If you have let your shoes dry fully, it is time to add a finish coat. Be sure to use the right finish with the right paint.

Angelus leather paint is finished with an acrylic lacquer available in a matte, satin, gloss, or high gloss finish. Take a soft cloth and hold it to the opening of the bottle and wet the cloth with the finish. Then apply a very thin layer across the painted areas and let it dry. A thin layer needs about 5 minutes to dry. Then apply another layer and continue until you have applied 3 to 4 layers on the shoe.

Jacquard Lumiere and Neopaque paints are OK without a sealer, according to the manufacturer, although I would suggest a finish with Pledge® Premium Floor Finisher with Future® Shine. It's a five-minute job that protects your design.

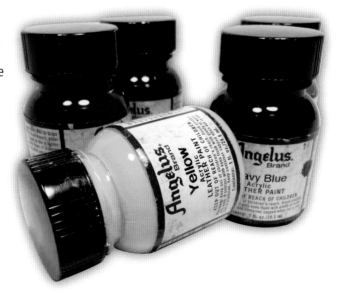

Grocery Lists: Supplies by Shoe Material

This section recaps the basic supplies necessary to decorate your shoes. The "necessary items" in each project specify the extras needed.

Canvas + Fabric Markers

- Washing machine/detergent
- Masking tape
- 4B pencil
- Flexible ruler
- Eraser and sharpener
- Fabric markers
- Fine and ultrafine black permanent markers
- Blow dryer or small iron system (like the quilt irons from Clover or Prym-Dritz)
- Old newspaper

Optional:
- Ribbons or laces to replace shoelaces
- Embellishments, dollmaking needle, and fisherman's thread (fishing line) or beading wire, glue
- Water repellent spray

Canvas + Fabric Paint

- Same as above PLUS
- Fabric paint instead of fabric markers
- 2 soft brushes: A small, straight-edge brush for larger areas and a small round brush for small details, lines, and correcting mistakes
- 2 jars of plain water: One for cleaning your brushes, one for correcting mistakes

Rubber or Vinyl or (Manmade) Leather + Permanent Markers

- A soft cloth and a little soap
- Kitchen towels, cotton swabs, and 70-95% alcohol for cleaning and emergency deleting
- Antibacterial hand sanitizer (with alcohol)
- Masking tape
- 600 grit sandpaper
- 4B pencil
- Flexible ruler
- Eraser and sharpener
- Permanent markers, optional with different tips
- Fine and ultrafine black permanent markers
- Old newspaper

Optional:
- Ribbons or laces to replace shoelaces
- Embellishments, dollmaking needle, and fisherman's thread (fishing line) or beading wire, glue

(Manmade) Leather + Leather Paint

- Acetone
- Lots of cotton wool
- Household gloves
- Protective mask
- Cotton swabs for the tiny edges
- Masking tape
- 4B pencil
- Flexible ruler
- Eraser and sharpener

Paint:

- Jacquard Lumiere and Neopaque paint for man-made leather and leather shoes OR
- Angelus leather paint for leather shoes. Do not mix both brands, especially for manmade leather.
- Tooth pick, or if you do not trust your nerves, an ultrafine permanent marker in black
- 3 soft brushes: A small straight-edge brush for lining large areas, a fan brush for filling large areas, and a tiny round brush for details
- 2 jars of plain water, one for cleaning your brushes, one for correcting mistakes. Replace the last one when used. Replace the first one regularly.
- Old newspaper

Paint:

For Angelus leather paint:
- Acrylic lacquer
- Soft cloth

For Jacquard Lumiere and Neopaque paint:
- Pledge Premium Floor Finisher with Future Shine
- Soft cloth

Optional:

- Ribbons or laces to replace laces
- Embellishments, glover's needle, fisherman's thread (fishing line) or beading wire, glue

How to Decorate Shoes

Now that you know everything about what to use to decorate, you need to know how to decorate your shoe. After preparation, your shoe is stripped of all the chemicals and you have created a base on which to sketch the pattern of your choice.

The decorating part of the process is one to take time for. This is your base ground, and if you do this part carefully, the next stage will be a kindergarten job—coloring inside the lines. After coloring and finishing, you can start embellishing with beads, buttons, and charms. And don't forget the shoelaces!

Pattern

Before drawing a design on a shoe, you will have to decide which pattern will suit the shoe. A pattern is based on a baseline or focal point, just like a quilt. In a medallion quilt, a focal point is used (the medallion) to attract your eye. With a traditional block quilt, the base line is a horizontal or vertical line around which the pattern is created.

Now your background is predefined (the shoe), and a natural baseline to work from might already exist, like a seam, stitching, or a shape on the shoe. You might want to base the pattern on that existing baseline. If you decide to create a pattern on a shoe without making use of a natural baseline, you need to create a baseline yourself.

Note: *All patterns in this book can be used on all kinds of shoes. However, a pattern based on a natural baseline may have to be adapted more than another pattern.*

There are several steps to building up the different patterns on a shoe. Some are quite simple and only need a focal point and a template. More advanced patterns need a self-constructed baseline, and the very advanced need a grid based on that self-created baseline or one that is built up around a baseline or shape of the shoe itself. In the next paragraphs, a guide is given for how to build up a pattern from the starting point.

To put the pattern on the shoe, use a very soft sharp pencil, preferably 4B (if not available, a #1 pencil). The pressure of your hand on the pencil should be light, just leaving a small trace to indicate where to work. This pencil line is erasable on leather, manmade leather, and vinyl using a cotton swab and alcohol. On fabric, a soft eraser does the trick, although a lot of erasing will grey your fabric. Also, your erasing should be light handed. If you plan on erasing a lot, be sure to use opaque paint. The pencil lines of the pattern will be the contour lines in your pattern and made black after coloring. Any pencil marks will be disguised in this way.

Chalk paper is also used by some to draw the outlines of a pattern on shoes. However, in my experience, the chalk will spread and vanishes easily during painting. My design was lost before I was able to color it. A ballpoint pen is used by some on leather and removed by acetone or the Angelus Preparer-Deglazer. I found out a ballpoint pen can influence the condition of the leather by leaving marks or even scratches.

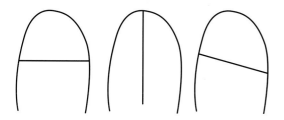

Where to Start?

Necessary supplies:
- 4B pencil (if not available a #1)
- Pencil sharpener
- Eraser
- Flexible ruler
- Old newspapers or paper

When you choose your design, look at how the design is built up. It might look like a random pattern, but it might also look like a grid, e.g., a Log Cabin (page 63). All patterns in the book make use of a focal point, most of them also a baseline (be it a natural or a self-created one); only one project uses a complete square grid, Log Cabins Afoot.

Before starting to draw, fill your shoes with a ball of paper to create a sturdy surface.

Whatever the pattern, keep one basic rule in mind—horizontal lines create a wider look, vertical lines a longer look, and diagonal lines make your shoe look narrower.

Because wide shoes usually make a shoe look plump, the patterns in this book are based on a diagonal and sometimes a vertical line. Horizontal lines are avoided when possible.

The Power of Flexible Rulers

To get a straight line on a shoe, a flexible ruler is there to help you. In patchwork, appliqué, and quilting, the flexible ruler is used to design a curved line on a straight surface. With shoe decoration, the flexible ruler is used reversed, to design a straight line on a curved surface.

Be sure to have a narrow and stable ruler that's able to follow the curves of your shoes and also has some stability itself. Working on a canvas shoe with a very floppy ruler may give you insufficient steadiness to draw a straight line. A too-rigid ruler will not follow the curve of the shoe, and you may end up with a crooked or wonky line.

How to Decorate Shoes

Creating a Focal Point

Every pattern, whatever the style, needs a focal point. For some patterns it is enough to start with this focal point. In most cases the focal point is on the middle on the upper of the shoe. One of the projects based on the focal point on this spot is the Flower Power

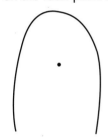

project (page 35). The point is to find the spot on the shoe where another person would look first. Put the shoe in front of you and just pinpoint the dot. Usually that's here:

One pattern in this book is based on a focal point on the side of the shoe—Portuguese Dinnerware (page 44). On that shoe the focal point is the center of the flower on the side of the shoe. Building up the pattern from that point creates a different angle to the shoe and may spice up a simple pattern.

Creating a Vertical Baseline

Some patterns only need one baseline, usually vertical. Hawaiian Retreat (page 49) and Mariner's Compass (page 47) projects are examples of this technique, which is applicable for all single decoration patterns.

First, find the focal point of the shoe. Then, take a flexible ruler and lay it vertically from the middle front top of the shoe right through the focal point to the nose of the shoe where you expect to find approximately the middle of your second toe, the one next to the big toe. This is the vertical line on which your single decoration pattern is centered.

The next step is to put the pattern on the right spot. If your pattern is a circle, then the middle of the circle is on the focal point, and the diameter of the circle is in line with this baseline. That 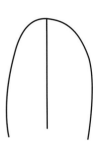 might not sound important, but when dealing with a vertical line in a circle, as with a Mariner's Compass, the baseline helps you center the pattern correctly.

A square pattern also has its center on the focal point. If you want to place the square on point, two opposite corners of the pattern square are on the baseline. Placing a square straight on a shoe creates a horizontal line that makes your shoe optically wider. If that's the effect you want to create, place the middle of the square on the focal point and two opposite sides of the square at a 90-degree angle to the baseline. Then you are sure the pattern is placed on the focal point of the shoe.

Creating a Diagonal Baseline and a Grid

There are several projects in this book where the pattern on the shoe is based on a full or partial grid. Check Patchwork Tootsies (page 40), Log Cabins Afoot (page 63), Clamshell Central (page 53), and

26

Hexagons on the Run (page 56). To create the grid to follow, you need a flexible ruler and a 4B pencil.

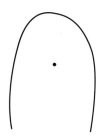

First, find the focal point of your shoe. The following step will be your basic design line. Take your flexible ruler and put the ruler diagonally over your shoe. Draw a line with pencil from the outside to the inside of the shoe, just following your ruler. Do not worry

if on the sides your line is not fully straight; make it as straight as possible. You will have to adapt your grid to the curves of your shoe anyway. Now you have your diagonal baseline.

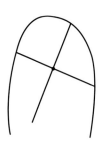

Then lay your ruler at a 90-degree angle on the baseline through the focal point. Draw this line, which is called the perpendicular. It depends on the kind of pattern whether you draw the line completely or just a short helpline.

In case you want a pattern with a full square grid (when creating blocks like Log Cabin), the line needs to be drawn fully from top to sole.

A repetitive pattern like the one on Clamshell Central or a more irregular grid like the one on Patchwork Tootsies doesn't need a full perpendicular. It's sufficient to have a helpline cross your baseline with 1" on each side.

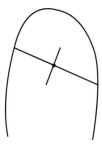

Repeat this perpendicular line on the right and the left side of your first perpendicular.

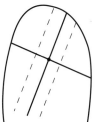

Be sure to follow the pattern. If your grid will be built up from 1" squares, the repeated perpendicular lines need to be at 1". If your grid is based on a repeated template like a coin or a hexagon, the perpendicular lines and the width between them need to be based on that template.

The next step is to repeat the baseline. With the help of the perpendicular lines, you can measure from the baseline directly on the perpendicular line where your

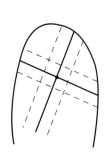

repeated baselines should be. As with the perpendicular lines, if your grid is 1" square, repeat the baseline at 1" on each side. If your grid is based on a template, base the repetition on the baseline.

For a full square grid, repeat both the perpendicular and the base lines until your shoe has a full grid. Because of the curves of the shoe, you will never create a perfectly square grid all over. Especially the little toe area and the area between the fourth and third toe are usually quite curved. There your grid will be bent as if a piece of fabric is pushed together.

Another example is the pattern on Flying Geese (page 51), which is based on the shape of the shoe itself. With sandals like these, following the shoe shape by drawing the line exactly in the middle and using the width of the upper to draw the Flying Geese makes the pattern follow the shoe.

Creating Your Own Pattern

With the help of these basics, you could try to design your own pattern. Be creative, truth or dare!

First, sketch what you like on paper. Don't worry whether you are or are not the next Van Gogh or Rembrandt; it's just a sketch. Any patchwork pattern can be put on a shoe as long as you keep your graphics steady.

> **Fact:** *The second shoe will never be the same. Just start with point 0 and use the same shape and colors. Your shoes will look like a pair, because they are alike.*

Creating a Pattern Around a Baseline or the Shoe Shape

A shoe might have its own baseline, a so-called natural baseline, which makes it possible to build up the pattern from there. Great examples are canvas basketball shoes such as Converse. The stitched line next to the eyelets is a great starting point to build up a feather or a swirl. A pattern that uses this baseline is Feathers on Parade (page 59).

Coloring and Contouring

Now that your pattern is on the shoe with pencil, your next step is coloring. The choice of the paint or the markers is based on the material of the shoe, as discussed in General Instructions (pages 8-23).

Plan your details and start with the light colors. That way your white flowers will not be covered with green grass before you think of them. Your color scheme can be chosen on the basis of the clothes in your wardrobe, but also on the colors of your favorite quilt. How about making hexagon shoes in the same color as the quilt you just finished?

If you are not sure whether the colors will be pleasing, work out the colors on paper or on a piece of fabric. Don't forget that leaving areas white or a very light pastel gives air and depth to your design, and makes it less heavy. Color all over in strong hues will make the contrast too big or nonexistent. Just like making a quilt!

Try to color inside the lines. A wavy edge alongside the pencil line and tiny spots crossing it are not an issue. When the pencil line is disguised with a black line, tiny flaws will be covered.

After you finish the coloring, the black contour lines are drawn. All pencil lines are covered with black after this stage. This black line gives contour for defining your design at a longer distance. If you have a very fine design, like Feathers on Parade (page 59), use an ultrafine tip. In all other cases, a fine marker will also cover the tiny flaws and any pencil lines.

Now that you are finished with the coloring, check how to finish your shoe in General Instructions (pages 8-23).

Embellishment

Your shoes are prepared, colored, and finished. The embellishments are the fringe benefits that give your shoes that extra something you will hardly find in any shoe store shoes. Be creative in what to put on your shoes, and keep in mind where you want to use your shoes. In a formal office area you might go somewhat less eccentric than on your quilt retreat with your friends of 20 years.

Some embellishments can be sewn on; others have to be glued on. Keep in mind that the uppers of your shoes are not a stable surface. The upper bends, it gets kicked, and somebody might even be so rude as to step on your toes. A simple sewing thread or a general purpose glue does not hold well enough to keep your shoe's embellishments attached.

Sewing on embellishments is preferred above gluing because of the direct and sturdier attachment to the shoe. For sewing on embellishments, use a very flexible and strong nylon beading wire or fisherman's thread (fishing line). Fisherman's thread is the most invisible and strongest option.

If you want the color to show and you are working on canvas shoes, you might choose a heavy duty polyester quilting thread such as Coats & Clark® Dual Duty®. Use a long sharp needle, such as 3½"

Piecemakers® dollmaking needles to reach the top of your toes and have a full and firm grip. A pair of tongs might help you to pull the needle through.

If something has to be glued on, like ribbons or lace, check out the material it's made from and the material you're gluing to. That defines the glue that needs to be used. Choose a flexible glue that will not discolor your embellishments. Your local hardware or craft store can help you out.

I do not recommend super glue. Super glue may discolor your fabric and is not flexible, so your embellishments will eventually break off.

How to Decorate Shoes

Shoelaces

Shoelaces are your first start when using shoes with eyelets such as general gym shoes or basketball shoes. The simple white ties can be replaced with a pair of closures that suit your design. If the shoes are for show, and you expect not to walk on them for hours, a yard of ribbon per shoe is a great shoelace. Colored ribbon or a golden cord makes your shoes extra attractive.

If your shoe needs a more sturdy closure, buy a pair of colored shoelaces. Check out the color that suits your shoe. You might not end there. Buy two yards of rickrack ribbon and attach it to the laces. Also, yarn or any other ribbon brings some spring in your step.

Finally, end up with some light beads at the ends of your shoelaces. A too-heavy bead may untie the knot unintentionally.

Beads and Buttons

Beads and buttons can be put on your shoes in several places, but to keep your shoes usable, put them on the upside of the upper of your shoe. Otherwise, you may get caught behind something which might damage your shoe.

For beginners, start with beads and buttons on canvas shoes. It is possible to sew them on (manmade) leather shoes, but you might want to get more experienced before trying that.

For canvas shoes, use a long sharp needle and a very sturdy, polyester quilting thread. Here is a step-by-step guide to making a sturdy attachment:

1. Make a triple or quadruple thread strand. Do not make a knot at the end of the thread.

2. Decide where you want to sew on the bead or the button and go in the shoe from above, exactly where you want the middle of the bead or the button. If there is a lining on the inside of the shoe, do not go through the lining, but keep at the outer layer of material.

3. Come back to the surface $1/16$" further and start with a surgeon's knot on that particular spot.

4. If the picture is not clear, an animated example can be found on www.quiltingthetownred.com/tutorials.

5. One end of the knot will be the strand you will be sewing with; the other end has to be hidden. Do not cut the latter and make it too short. You have to leave a long-enough strand to be able to thread your needle with it, tie another knot, and then stitch it away. A length of 4"–5" should be enough. Leave it for now.

6. Next, thread your needle with the long strand and start sewing on the button or the bead. When finished, come up from below, and stay between your embellishment and the upper of the shoe.

7. Make another surgeon's knot with both strands (the long strand and the strand from step 5 you left behind).

8. Both strands are hidden by stitching them away. If there is a lining, thread your needle, go down in the leather under the embellishment, and end up further inside the shoe. You can cut the strand inside the shoe and hide the strand between the lining and the leather.

If there is no lining, thread your needle with both strands (make sure the eye of the needle is large enough), circle two times around the attachment of the embellishment and then cross it three times from left to right and back until tight. Do not go to the upside of the embellishment or under the leather. Now you can cut off the excess strands. For extra security, put a little glue on the ends of the strands to attach them to the knot.

Be careful not to leave the knot or unfinished loose ends on the inside of the shoe. Your feet might get irritated by the tiny bump or the sharp ends.

Tying beads and buttons on leather shoes requires the use of flexible nylon beading thread or fishing line with a high knot strength and sturdy gloves and needles. A pair of pliers and a special thimble will help you get through the leather. Follow the rest of the instructions for sewing on canvas.

Crystals

Crystals are a great way to decorate a shoe. However, the upper of your shoe is a flexible area. A single crystal on (manmade) leather or canvas upper is a great idea, but when you really want to apply a whole bunch of crystals, check out more stable areas such as the heels. Use a hot-fix applicator or Gem-Tac (an adhesive by Beacon®) for a sturdy fix.

Crystals are not suitable for long term wear on vinyl or rubber shoes; the glue does not mix with the rubber but melts in, so there is no firm attachment. One less-than-elegant dance partner and the whole crystal pattern on your toes is gone.

However, fabric does attach to rubber and vinyl with the right glue. As a workaround, you can glue your crystal pattern onto fabric, and then glue the fabric to the rubber or vinyl. For the crystals, use a hot-fix applicator or Gem-Tac; for the fabric, use a flexible glue for attaching fabric to rubber or vinyl.

How to Decorate Shoes

Ribbons, Lace, and Fabric

Ribbons and lace can give your shoes that just-so-special and very personal look. Because we walk outside and shoes get dirty, I usually apply ribbons and lace only to shoes that can be washed. Use ribbons and laces to weave through the holes of your Crocs, or glue them on your Toms as in Ribbon City (page 38). A bow tie on the front or back of your shoe gives pizzazz.

Stitching is a great option for ribbon and lace and demands a sturdy polyester quilting thread. Use a sharp dollmaking needle and a hem stitch to stitch the ribbon onto your canvas shoes. If there is a lining, stay between the lining and the upper when going under the canvas to prevent your feet from feeling the stitches.

Some brands, however, do have glue between the canvas and the lining that will make your needle become tacky within a few stitches. When working with larger pieces of fabric, stitching is also not an option. Gluing is then a better method.

Use a textile-to-textile glue and spread it thinly on the fabric according to the manufacturer's directions. A specialized glue will not discolor the ribbon or the canvas and will stay flexible for years. Your basketball shoes can be refurbished with the fabric of your choice, or, you can make a collage of ribbons, lace, and fabric to create a Victorian crazy quilt on your shoes!

Projects

Flower Power

This pair of shoes is especially suitable for your first try using fabric or paint markers on textiles. Using the foam stickers or paper shapes for the pattern makes it easy to create your design. The technique is simple and results in a very individual pair of shoes!

Necessary items:

- For preparation, coloring, and finishing materials, see General Instructions (pages 8-23)
- White or light colored shoes
- Foam stickers of flowers, hearts, and dots or paper shapes to trace, see Resources

Color scheme:

Lime green, purple, blue, light blue, red, orange, gold, yellow

1. Clean your shoes. Let your shoes dry before starting the next step.

2. The side of the sole will not be decorated. Put masking tape around the sole to keep it free from paint.

3. Start designing. Create the focal point on your shoe.

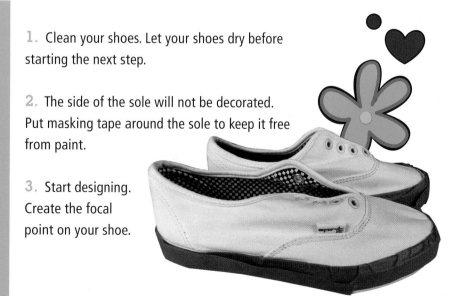

35

Flower Power

4. Take a foam sticker and put it on the shoe on the focal point. Trace the sticker with a pencil and remove the sticker. The first shape is now on your shoe. Add other shapes at will.

5. Play with your shapes. Make the eyelets the center of a flower, or just put flowers everywhere, not following any line of the shoe. A flower can even cross stitching if you want it to. This design is very free, and is a great way to experiment with shapes and color.

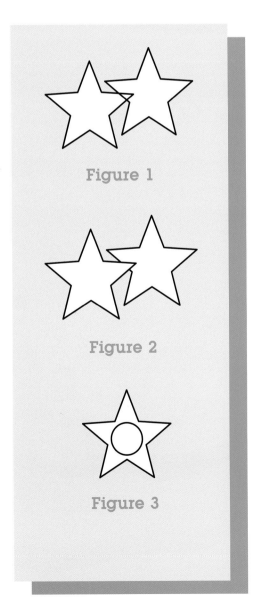

Figure 1

Figure 2

Figure 3

6. Start tracing shape upon shape on your shoe, until your shoe is filled.

7. To get depth in your design, place some shapes only partially on a designated spot. Remember, visually, your second shape is always behind your first shape. If the new shape is completely within the lines of your first shape, you can put the second shape up front.

Look at these examples:

Figure 1: The second shape is traced on the first shape. The point of the first shape is still visible. There is no order here in back or front.

Figure 2: The second shape is only traced where the other star is not visible, only next to it. Depth is created because the second star is now behind the first star.

Figure 3: The second shape is put completely within the lines of the star. Now the circle is in front and the star is behind it.

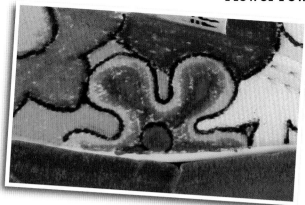

8. Now start coloring! Just color inside the lines. Start with the lighter colors and just keep coloring. One color will be your background color, and for contrast, it's better to not use that color in a shape. In the example pair, lime is the background.

9. Specify the colors you want to use and stick to that scheme. That makes it easier to decorate the second shoe in a similar way.

10. When you use markers, experimenting with color lines may give great results. Building color in a shape by using lines of color results in a rainbow, and working layer upon layer creates shadow. If you want to practice first, take a piece of paper and experiment. There is no wrong way.

11. The background is done last. Fill in spaces between shapes with the color you have decided to use as your background. When you have finished coloring the shapes and the background, cover the pencil lines with a black permanent marker.

12. Add embellishments (see How to Decorate Shoes, pages 24-32). The example pair has ribbon for laces.

Ribbon City

The Ribbon City project is the easiest way of decorating canvas shoes. This is a great project for a bee or a guild program. Take your Toms or other canvas shoes, some ribbons and buttons to a meeting, and you walk out with your own pair! This pattern is for canvas shoes only.

1. Start decorating your cleaned, dry shoes with ribbons. Check how long the ribbon should be to put it on the spot where you want it on your shoe. Take a bit extra at both ends of the ribbon. Attach the beginning of the ribbon to itself with a tiny bit of glue to prevent fraying. Pin the ribbon to the shoes so you are certain how long the ribbon should be. To measure the length for an elastic area, stretch the elastic area and measure the needed length. Fold back the extra bit at the end of the ribbon and glue it to itself, so you end up with a ribbon that's exactly the perfect size.

Necessary items:
- Canvas shoes, prewashed and dried
- Pins
- Ribbons or lace
- Textile glue (Fabri-tac or something similar)
- Buttons
- Dollmaking needle
- Thread (beading thread, fishing line, or, for less-stressed areas, Coats & Clark Dual Duty)
- Pair of scissors

Color scheme:
White and red

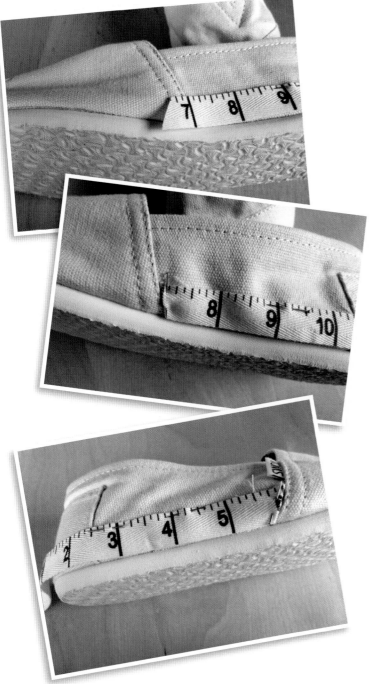

When both ends are dry, glue the ribbon to its spot. Be gentle with the amount of glue. Too much glue will pour through the ribbon and make stains. Do not glue on an elastic area, as your ribbon is non-elastic. The example pair has measuring tape ribbon—quite clever for a quilter's footwear.

2. Put on as many ribbons as you want. Before you start with the buttons, let the glue dry.

3. Pin your buttons in place where you want them attached.

4. Take your needle and thread and attach the buttons with a surgeon's knot (see page 30). Be sure to secure the ends by hiding them in the knot or under the fabric. As Toms are lined, hiding the ends is easy between the outer fabric and the lining.

Enjoy your personalized Toms!

Patchwork Tootsies

This pattern is great for your first adventure working with color. With permanent markers you have every patch to experiment with patterns, textures, and details. And while you are becoming more experienced, paint will give you even more options.

Fun, bright, comfortable, and individual, these clogs are terrific because no pair will look the same. Your clogs will look like they are made from different fabrics. The technique is based on the self-created baseline (see General Instructions, pages 8-23).

Necessary items:

- 1 pair of white clogs
- For preparation, coloring, and finishing materials, see General Instructions (pages 8-23)

Color scheme:

Every color in the book!

1. Clean your clogs. Make sure your shoes are dry before starting the next stage.

2. Mark the focal point. Draw a line with pencil from the outside to the inside of the shoe, just following your ruler. Do not worry if your line on the sides is not fully straight; the start and end of your baseline will be erased anyway with this design.

3. To start your design distribution, build up the position of your blocks with "fabric" over the shoe. You will still able to erase what you've drawn.

> ***To get a better division of the patches on the shoe, here are some basics:***
> - *There is no line, including the baseline, that goes straight from one side to the other side of the shoe or from the toe to the tip.*
> - *Straight lines make your shoes look bigger; broken lines, smaller.*
> - *Keep your patches big, to be able to create texture and design in the patches.*

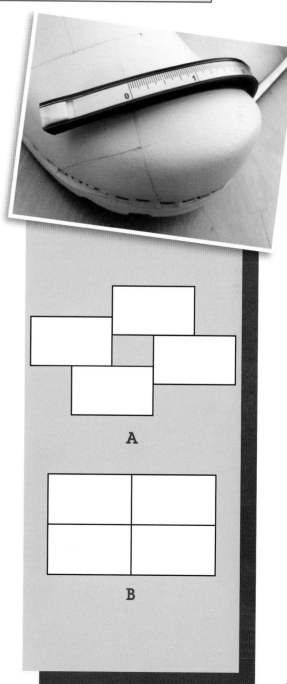

4. Take your flexible ruler and put it in a 90-degree angle (round and about) on the baseline through your focal point and draw a short perpendicular line. Then draw a line about 1" further down the perpendicular parallel to the basic line to the outside of your shoe. Repeat the perpendicular line 1" further to form a rectangle. The first patch on the outside top of your shoe is there.

5. Now, use your eraser and erase the top of the line from the top to the toe, until you reach the baseline. There, you stop. Then 2" further on that baseline, draw another line to the top of your shoe. Each time you draw lines, be sure that you make no long array of patches, but make your lines go like A instead of like B.

Arrange patches that do link, but you should never have 4 patches linking on 1 corner. After drawing and erasing a few times, your shoe will have an array of rectangles spread over the shoe.

A

B

Patchwork Tootsies

6. Grab your markers or your paint and start coloring your patches. Now the fun of choosing your colors starts. Start with the lightest colors, finish with the darkest. A darker paint or marker may hide a slight error with a lighter color; that's not the case the other way around.

7. Fill all your patches with the textures of your choice, and stay within your pencil lines. The end result looks something like this.

8. Fill the patches with all kinds of fabric structures and details such as hearts and flowers.

9. Making your stitches has never been easier! Use your black fine permanent marker. Draw a black line around each patch, following the pencil lines you drew before. After that, start making your stitches: small lines with your fine black marker with a 90-degree angle on your black marker lines to form small hem stitches.

Your first shoe is ready, now for the second!

42

Note: *If there's one lesson to be learned with designing your own shoes, it is that you can never make the same shoe again. Not even the second of a pair. If you know that, you can make a pair, without making them the same.*

10. Start with the second shoe the same way as with your first one. *Don't look at the first shoe,* just draw your lines the same free way you did with the first one.

11. When you start with coloring, take your first shoe and *look at the fabrics you created with your paint or the markers. These fabrics you are going* to remake on your second shoe. So, if you made a pink fabric with red hearts on the first shoe, make it again on the second shoe. Not on the same area of the shoe, but somewhere in one of the patches. Did you create a checkered green fabric on the toe? Create it again on one of the side patches.

You will probably not have the same amount of patches on the second shoe as on the first shoe. Usually it differs by one or two. You might decide to create, double, or skip a fabric. As long as most of the "fabrics" are recreated, you will create a viable pair of shoes.

12. Finish the shoes as described in General Instructions.

Portuguese Dinnerware

T

This project is based on a pot cover I found in a cupboard at a friend's house. Inspiration is everywhere!

The focal point of the shoe is on the front side of the shoe. By building up the design from there, step by step, you create your own personal pair. The colors make it look like Portuguese dinnerware.

Necessary items:
- White or light colored shoes
- Two copies of patterns on page 71
- Pins (for canvas shoes)
- Tracing paper
- For preparation, coloring and finishing materials, check the grocery list in General Instructions (pages 22-23).

Color scheme:
Warm yellow, blue, light blue, blue-green, red, orange, and gold

When working with leather:
White

1. Clean your shoes. Let them dry before starting the next step.

2. While your shoes are drying, copy patterns A and B on page 71 twice (one for each shoe).

The shape and size of your shoes and your own personal idea define how large the pattern should be. If you want a big flower covering the whole front of your shoe, or a smaller one on the side, you can use your copy machine and your template to work out the size that's best for you by enlarging or reducing its size.

When you have decided what the size should be, cut out the templates. Pattern A is for the front of your shoe; pattern B is for the heel of your shoe.

For a first trial, drawing pattern B on the shoe heel is a great start. It makes you familiar with the pattern, the outlines, and the work order. Cut out the copied pattern and trace the lines with a pencil. The excess of graphite will be your markings on the shoe.

Put the back of the shoe in front of you. The seam on the back is your middle line. If there is no seam on the back, imagine a straight vertical line from the top of your shoe to the center of your back heel. Pin or tape the pattern to the heel of the shoe with the traced pattern to the surface of the shoe.

Rub the backside of the pattern with a pencil to transfer the pattern to the surface of the shoe. Draw pattern B on the second shoe. You may also choose to transfer only the main lines. This is an easier option when the template needs adaptations or the surface of your shoe is unsteady.

Portuguese Dinnerware

3. Start drawing pattern A on the shoe. Choose a focal point on the shoe on the front side. That is where the middle of your flower will be. The pattern is transferred to the shoe like pattern B.

The only thing that is important is that the center of the heart of the flower is exactly on the focal point on your shoe. After that, it is pinning or taping the pattern to the shoe and rubbing it off.

You may choose to transfer all lines at once, or to transfer only the main lines and fill in details by drawing, like I did. The latter gives you the option to adapt the design to your shoe. It might well be that you will not need the full pattern. The pattern is made larger to fit on any shoe. Draw the second shoe.

4. Color the pattern. The side of the sole will not be decorated, so put masking tape around the sole to keep it free from paint.

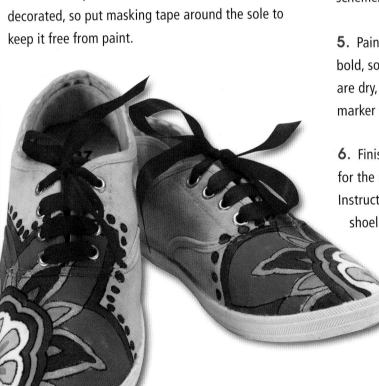

To create the color scheme of the sample Portuguese Dinnerware project, the background of the shoe is a warm yellow. Of course, you might also take the colors of your own choice. Coloring first on a copy of the pattern may help to develop the right color scheme.

5. Paint or use a marker. The pattern is set up to be bold, so it's just a matter of filling in. When the shoes are dry, cover the pencil lines with a black ultrafine marker to add contrast.

6. Finish the shoe according to the description for the material you're working on, see General Instructions (pages 8-23). Find a pair of great shoelaces or make them yourself from ribbons or stitch rickrack onto laces. I left it at that, but you might think about adding beads or charms. Go ahead, they're yours!

Decorate Your Shoes • Annemart Berendse

Mariner's Compass

The Mariner's Compass is a difficult pattern to make in a quilt, and whole books have been written about it. However, it is less difficult to draw a Mariner's Compass pattern on a shoe. It just a matter of transferring it!

Necessary items:

- White or light colored shoes
- Tracing paper
- Pins (for canvas shoes)
- Tape (for manmade and natural leather, rubber, or vinyl)
- For preparation, coloring, and finishing materials, check the grocery lists, pages 22-23.

Color scheme:

Yellow, light blue, navy, red, blue-green (when working with markers both light and dark)

When working on leather:

White

1. Clean your shoes. Let them dry before starting the next step.

2. Trace the compass pattern, the star pattern, and the fleur-de-lys pattern from page 72 onto tracing paper. Don't be gentle with your pencil; push it a bit extra to get an overdose of pencil marks. Cut out the pattern with a generous margin.

3. Push a pin from the back to the front of the paper on the end of one of the compass points. Then do the same with the exact opposite point. These points will be your North and South and will be your helpline to get the pattern exactly on the shoe's vertical baseline. Finally, push a pin from back to front in the exact center of your pattern. That point will be exactly on your focal point. Put your transfers aside for step 5.

Mariner's Compass

4. Draw a vertical baseline and mark the focal point in the middle on the top of your shoe. Place a dot there by pinpointing it with pencil.

Then take a flexible ruler and lay it vertically from the middle front top of the shoe, right through the focal point to the nose of the shoe where you expect to find approximately the middle of your second toe, the one next to the big toe. This is the vertical line on which your decoration pattern is centered. Draw that line, lightly, and only just a bit longer than the area where your pattern will be placed. For help, check General Instructions, pages 8-23.

5. Transfer the patterns to the shoe using the transfers from step 2. The compass pattern will be put upside down on the shoe to transfer the pencil markings onto it. Push the pin (or press the tape) that is in the center of the pattern into the focal point. Then push the pins (or tape) that are on the North and South points of your pattern exactly on the vertical baseline. The paper must be flat, not stretched to fit.

Take your pencil and color the back of the pattern, or rub the paper gently against the fabric, so the excess of the pencil markings on the front of the pattern are transferred to the fabric. A sturdy paper ball in your shoe or a hand placed inside the shoe helps to put extra pressure on the pattern. When you remove the paper, the pattern should be visible on the shoe.

For the stars and the fleur-de-lys, trace the patterns on paper and transfer them by rubbing or coloring the back of the paper. Make multiple transfers for the several stars on the shoes.

Draw the patterns on the other shoe.

6. Color the shoe according to the example color scheme or develop your own. When working with paint, to make a darker blue-green, just add a tip of navy to your regular blue-green. If markers are your coloring devices, you will need two different markers, as blending with markers is generally more difficult.

7. When finished coloring, let the shoe dry. Then cover the pencil lines with an ultrafine black marker.

8. Finish the shoe according to its material (see General Instructions).

Hawaiian Retreat

These sandals have been transformed from plain white to the perfect retreat slippers.

1. Clean your sandals. Let them dry before starting the next step.

2. Trace the pattern from page 72 onto tracing paper. Don't be gentle with your pencil; push it a bit extra to get an overdose of pencil marks. Cut out the pattern with a generous margin.

3. Push a pin from the back to the front of the paper on the end of one of the design points. Then do the same with the exact opposite point. These points will be your North and South and will be your help line to get the pattern exactly on the sandal's vertical baseline. Finally push a pin from back to front in the exact center of your pattern. That point will be exactly on your focal point. Put your transfers aside for step 5.

Necessary items:
- White or light-colored sandals
- Tracing paper
- Pins (for canvas sandals)
- Tape (for manmade and natural leather, rubber, and vinyl sandals)
- For preparation, coloring, and finishing materials, see General Instructions, pages 8-23.

Color scheme:
Gold, navy, turquoise

When working with Angelus leather paint:
Yellow

Hawaiian Retreat

Note: *When working with (manmade) leather, rubber, or vinyl, use masking tape instead of pins.*

4. Draw a vertical baseline and mark the focal point in the middle on the top of your sandal. Place a dot there by pinpointing it with pencil.

Then take a flexible ruler and lay it vertically from the middle front top of the sandal, right through the focal point to the nose of the upper where you expect to find approximately the middle of your second toe, the one next to the big toe. This is the vertical line on which your decoration pattern is centered. Draw that line, lightly and only just a bit longer than the area where your pattern will be placed. For help, see General Instructions, pages 8-23.

5. Transfer the pattern to the sandal using the transfers from step 2. Lay the square with the pattern upside down with two opposite points on the vertical baseline. Fix the pattern to the sandal with a little masking tape at the sides of the pattern. Leave the corners of the square free. The paper must be flat, not stretched to fit. Take your pencil and color the back of the pattern, or rub the paper gently against the material, so the excess of the pencil markings on the front of the pattern are transferred to the fabric. A hand placed inside the upper helps to put extra pressure on the pattern.

Place four dots on the upper on the exact points of the corners of the square of your pattern. The square is on point on the sandal.

When you remove the paper, the pattern and the four dots should be visible. Connect the four dots by using a flexible ruler and pencil to recreate the square.

Draw the pattern on the other sandal.

6. Color the pattern according to the color scheme or develop your own. When working with Angelus leather paint, color the parts you want to be gold with a few layers of yellow before applying gold.

7. When you have finished coloring, let the sandals dry. Then emphasize the Hawaiian cutout and the square in your pattern with an ultrafine black marker.

8. Finish the sandals according to the material (see General Instructions).

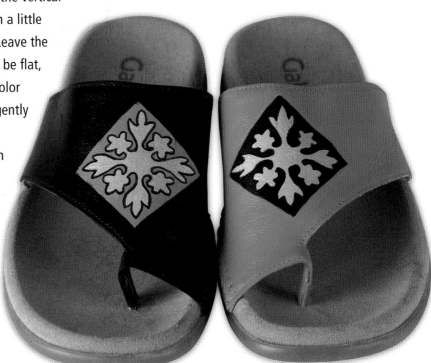

Flying Geese

These sandals have been transformed from plain white to the perfect retreat slippers. They are sparkly and bright in rainbow colors, but if you adapt the color scheme you might use pastels or even a fall color scheme.

Necessary items:
- White or light-colored sandals
- For preparation, coloring, and finishing materials, see General Instructions, pages 8-23.

Color scheme:
Aqua, red, orange, yellow, green, blue, and violet

1. Clean your sandals. Let them dry before starting the next step. Protect the soles with masking tape.

2. The baseline for this pattern is based on the shape of the sandal. To define the baseline, measure the sandal material from side to side with your flexible ruler and place a pencil dot exactly in the middle. By measuring on several spots, the dots will define a line. The area where the three straps of the sandal come together will be free and does not ask for a baseline. Check the pattern on page 71 for visual help.

3. The bottom lines of the geese triangles are the lines that are at a 90-degree angle to the base line from side to side of the strap of the sandal.

51

Flying Geese

Start at the side bottom strap of your sandal. Measure the width of the material, which will form the bottom line, with your flexible ruler. Divide it by two. That is the height of your triangle.

Place a dot on the baseline at the height of your triangle, measured from the triangle's bottom line. Take your ruler again and draw a new bottom line for the next triangle through the dot at a 90-degree angle to the baseline. Draw from the dot to the sides of the triangle. Check the pattern on page 71 for visual help. On the left side of this pattern is shown with dotted lines how to design the triangles.

Repeat the measuring of the triangle's bottom line, defining the height by dividing it in two and placing the dot on the baseline. The last dot that ends close to the middle of the front of the shoe does not need a new bottom line for the following triangle. Usually 6 to 7 triangles go on a side, depending on the size of the shoe and the width of the material. Particularly small straps like those on flip-flops might have many more but smaller triangles, all defined with the same method.

4. Take a soft eraser or a cotton swab with alcohol and remove the baseline in the middle.

5. Draw the pattern on the other sandal and remove the middle baseline.

6. Color the pattern according to the sample color scheme or develop your own. The example sandal color scheme follows the primary and secondary colors and develops a nice rainbow look.

7. When finished coloring, let the sandals dry. By outlining the triangles with an ultrafine or fine black marker, the contrast and color are emphasized.

8. Finish the sandals according to the material (see General Instructions).

Clamshell Central

Crocs are comfortable, but sometimes a bit plain. This pattern relates to the holes in the upper front with the circular pattern, and is also easily applicable to another type of shoe.

Remember, with rubber or plastic shoes like Crocs, the design will not last forever!

1. Clean your clogs. Protect the soles from coloring with masking tape. Let your shoes dry before starting the next step.

2. First, the template is prepared. Trace a $^7/_8$" circle and make 3 marks on the template with a permanent marker. The 3 marks are the North, the East, and the West of the circle. After this step your template should look like this:

The markings on the East and West help you place the template on the baseline. The North marking helps you to pinpoint the middle of the circle where the two circles above it should come together.

Necessary items:
- 1 pair of white Crocs or clogs
- A penny or other approximately $^7/_8$" diameter circle template
- For preparation, coloring, and finishing materials, see General Instructions, pages 8-23.

Color scheme:
Don't be afraid to grab every color you can find. I worked with: Yellow, sky blue, blue, orange, green, mint, red, pink, navy, and a black ultrafine permanent marker.

Clamshell Central

3. To be able to use the baseline, we have to create a focal point (front middle of the shoe) and draw the baseline. Put the shoe in front of you and mark the focal point with a pencil (see General Instructions).

4. To create the basic design line, put the flexible ruler diagonally over your shoe. A more horizontal or vertical setting will make your shoe look wider and longer. A diagonal setting will make it look smaller.

Draw a line with pencil from the outside to the inside of the shoe, sole to sole, just following your ruler. Do not worry if the line on the sides is not fully straight; the curves in your shoe prevent your line from being perfectly straight.

Repeat the line above and under the baseline by using your template.

Position the template with East and West on the baseline and pinpoint North on the shoe with a pencil. Do that several times so you only have to connect the dots by using your flexible ruler and your pencil. Go to the next step when you have at least 2 parallel lines to your baseline on your shoe. For more help on this, see General Instructions.

5. Put the East and West template marks on the baseline. Draw half a circle on the baseline, tracing the template. The line should now look something like this:

Repeat the half circles by using the marks on your template to position the Clamshell exactly next to the previous half circle. Because your shoe is curved, you might have to fiddle a bit. That's OK, as long as you keep the half circles staggered to create the pattern. After erasing your baselines, the pattern will look like this:

Decorate Your Shoes • Annemart Berendse

On Crocs I prefer to keep the Clamshells on the uppers and keep the rest of the shoe free of decoration to prevent shedding to my socks. You might decide to keep on going and fill the shoe completely.

Color the shoe according to the example color scheme or develop your own. It's best to spread similar colors across the shoe, so you won't have three yellow clamshells next to each other.

Decorate the second shoe.

When finished coloring, let the shoes dry. By outlining the shapes with an ultrafine or fine black marker, the contrast and color are emphasized.

Finish the shoe according to the material you're working on (see General Instructions).

Hexagons on the Run

T his pair is the same as the white leather Birkenstocks I used for my own first pair of decorated shoes. Plain, white, and nothing fancy. After a little creativity, the shoes look like a genuine pair of walking hexagons!

Necessary items:
- 1 pair of white shoes
- ½" hexagon template
- For preparation, coloring, and finishing materials, see General Instructions, pages 8-23.

Color scheme:
Yellow as a base for gold Angelus leather paint, then blue-green, blue, light blue, hot pink, violet, lilac, gold, and black ultrafine permanent marker

1. Clean your clogs. Let your shoes dry before starting the next step.

Template

2. To make the baseline to draw the hexagon pattern, first the template is prepared. Trace this pattern onto cardboard, or use standard paper-piecing hexagons, available in all sizes. A ½" hexagon is a great size for a shoe, but you might want to experiment with larger or smaller sizes. For my pair of shoes I used 12 templates. Hard plastic templates are not an option; your template needs to be flexible to follow the curves on your shoe.

Note: *Make or buy more templates, because after tracing a few times, the corners of the hexagons start to become rounded, and then your template is of no value anymore.*

3. To create a baseline, start with the focal point at the front middle of the shoe and mark that spot. Put your flexible ruler diagonally over your shoe. Draw a line from sole to sole across the shoe to have a starting point for the next lines.

4. To draw the next baselines, position the hexagon template with one corner on the focal point and the opposite corner on the baseline. Mark the upside and the downside of the hexagon. Repeat that on the same baseline. The result is a baseline for the hexagons yet to come on top of your hexagon by connecting the dots. Be gentle with your pencil; a lot of the lines will be removed later on.

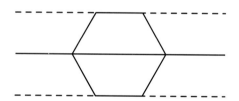

Now repeat this at the same baseline by positioning the template both completely above or under the baseline to create a secondary baseline by connecting the dots.

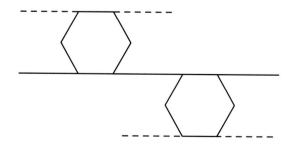

When fully done, you should have five baselines now: The baseline you started with, two baselines at half hexagon height above and under, and two at full hexagon height above and under.

Repeat the same building up of baselines by starting the same method from the above and the under full hexagon line. This line work is your helpline to position the hexagons. The baseline work is now finished. For more help, see General Instructions.

5. Position a hexagon template with one corner on the focal point and the opposite corner on the same baseline. Trace the hexagon. Your second hexagon is NOT directly next to it, but half a hexagon higher or lower.

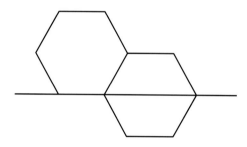

Repeat the tracing of the hexagons, by building them half up, half down, using your baselines as helplines. Because your shoe is curved, you might have to fiddle a bit. That's OK as long as you try to keep your hexagons connected from point to point.

There is one area where you will definitely have to end with a pentagon instead of a hexagon—the toe of your shoe. At the area around your big toe the curves are so steep that the hexagons will bend together and automatically form the shape of a small pentagon, one at the front, one at the side of your big toe. When that happens, accept it; do not try to solve it. There is no other way to position a shape based on 2 dimensions on a 3-dimensional area.

Hexagons on the Run

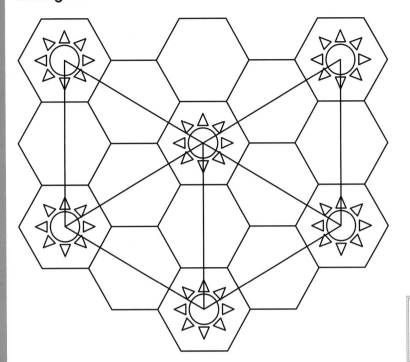

spread of the colors, I chose 7 per hexagon flower. I used gold as my centerpiece and repeated the color as if there were a large triangle of hexagons where the color has to be repeated.

The marked areas get the color you want them to have. This way none of the colors will end up next to each other.

Note: *Especially when working with leather paint, work in thin layers.*

The last step in this stage is outlining the hexagons with a fine or ultrafine black permanent marker.

6. After your shoe is full of hexagons, erase any baselines that are in the middle of full hexagons. The other part of the baseline should be a side of a hexagon. The strap of the shoe is not marked for decoration but will be colored in 1 color.

7. Decorate the second shoe.

8. Color the shoe according to the example color scheme or develop your own. To develop an even

9. Finish the shoe according to the material (see General Instructions).

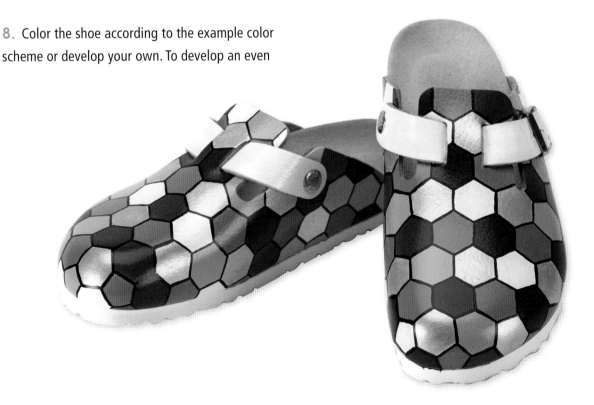

Decorate Your Shoes • Annemart Berendse

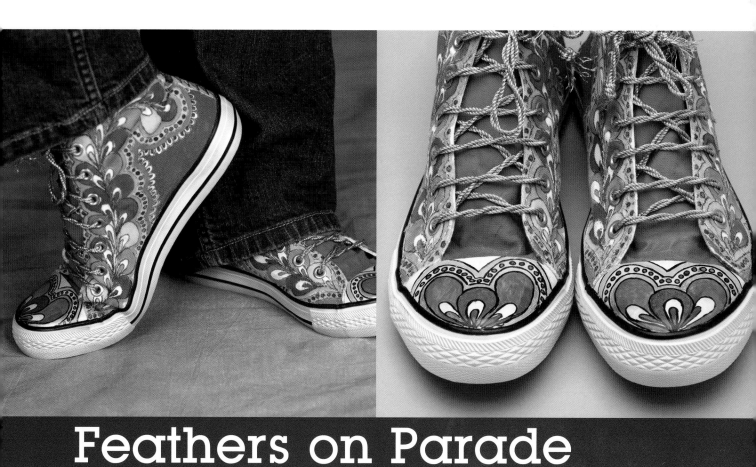

Feathers on Parade

Feathers on Parade is a real showoff project—a detailed design built on a very common baseball or basketball shoe. Although the design may look intricate, if you start from the baseline and work step by step, the pattern can be applied without too much difficulty.

Note: *It's important to keep your pencil sharp to be able to make the fine lines. Having a copy of the full pattern in front of you helps you to focus on the immediate stage of your drawing.*

Necessary items:

- 1 pair of white baseball or basketball shoes
- A penny or other approximately $7/8$" circle template
- Copies of the pattern
- Permanent markers in blue, red, black, green, purple, orange, and yellow for decoration of the shoe toe
- For preparation, coloring, and finishing materials, see General Instructions, pages 8-23.

Color scheme:

Orange, red, green, blue, purple, light blue, yellow, and gold

Feathers on Parade

1. Clean your shoes. Let them dry before starting the next step.

2. The baseline of the shoe is a natural line of the shoe; the line next to the eyelets is used to build up the design. The stitches of this line are the spine of the feather. The spine of the feather starts at the bottom, follows the stitches, and ends with a curl at the ankle. Draw this line with a sharp pencil. To experiment, make a copy of the plain shoe (page 73) and the shoe with spine (page 73) and draw on paper.

3. Now you are going to make your feathers. Take a coin that fits well between the spine of the feather and the border, and fit around the eyelet. A penny is usually a good size. There has to be some room left to add a line of ⅛" width. Make half circles on the outside, around the eyelets of the shoe.

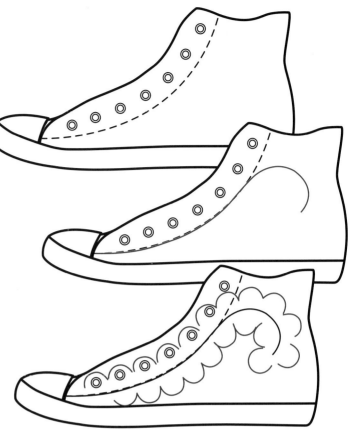

3a. Then connect the half circles to develop a feather. The upper line of the half circle is connected with the baseline at the height of the lower line of the half circle before. It sounds complicated, but this drawing helps make it clear:

Decorate Your Shoes • Annemart Berendse

3b. The next step is to draw a line around the feather at ⅛". Then draw two drops that fit within each other inside the feather blades. Draw tiny circles around the outer edge of the ⅛" ribbon around the feather and outline them with a line.

3c. Repeat a second outline. Then decorate the line with a line of double lace (see complete pattern on page 76). The drawing on the side of the shoe is now finished.

3d. Repeat the mirrored pattern on the other side of the shoe, and then both on the second shoe.

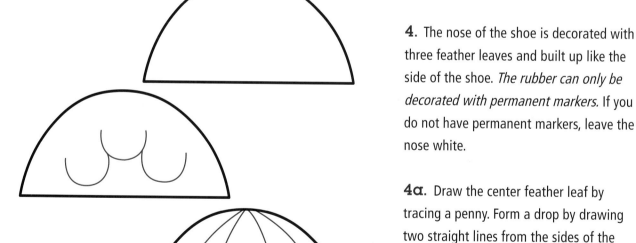

4. The nose of the shoe is decorated with three feather leaves and built up like the side of the shoe. *The rubber can only be decorated with permanent markers.* If you do not have permanent markers, leave the nose white.

4a. Draw the center feather leaf by tracing a penny. Form a drop by drawing two straight lines from the sides of the circle to the center of the nose of the shoe.

4b. Draw the two side leaves by tracing the penny template and forming a feather leaf by elongating the outer sides in a curved line to the center of the toe of the shoe. Fill the feather leaves with drops like the design on the outside of the shoe.

Feathers on Parade

4c. Outline the feather leaves with a ⅛" line, draw tiny circles outside the line, and repeat the outline at ⅛" twice. The finished drawing on the shoe toe should look like this now:

5. On the back of a basketball shoe there is generally a ¾" wide strip from the back heel to the top. That strip is filled with Flying Geese.

5a. Start at the base of the strip and measure the width. Half the width is the height of the triangle. Put a dot in the middle at the height of the triangle. Draw two diagonal lines from the base of the strip to the dot to form a triangle. At the height of the top of the triangle draw a horizontal line that forms the base of your next triangle. Fill the strip with triangles. The triangles are small. You might need to fiddle a bit to fill the whole strip with triangles. The best way to calculate that is to measure the width of the strip and then the length of the strip.

5b. Divide the length of the strip by the half width of the strip. Now you know how many triangles will be on the back. If the result of your division is a little bit above a whole number (say 6.3), you will have to make your triangles a little bit taller, so exactly 6 will fit in. If the result of your division is a little bit below a whole number (say 5.8), you will have to make your triangles a little bit shorter to fit in 6.

6. Color the textile part of the shoe according to the color scheme; let the shoe dry. Finish the coloring by outlining the design and thus covering the pencil lines with a black permanent marker. Outlining the triangles in ultrafine or fine lines will emphasize the contrast and color.

7. Color and outline the toe of the shoe.

8. Finish the shoe according to the material (see General Instructions), remembering that this project has two types of material to think about—canvas and rubber.

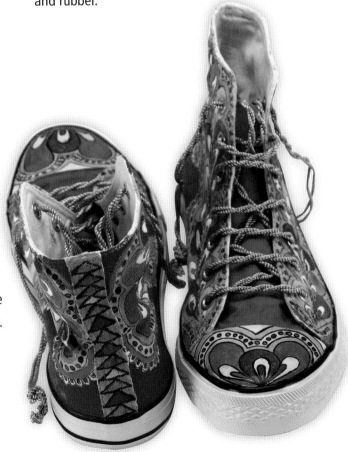

Log Cabins Afoot

The pattern on these clogs is based on a full grid. This means precision during the design process. After that, it gets easier. This project is a great blank canvas for a more refined clog, allowing you to make your own Log Cabin lay out. Make it bright, make it sophisticated, make it what you want to make it!

Necessary items:
- 1 pair of white shoes
- For preparation, coloring, and finishing materials, see General Instructions, pages 8-23.

Colors needed in paint or marker:

Yellow, sky blue, blue, lime, navy, and black ultrafine permanent marker

1. Clean your clogs. Let them dry before starting the next step.

2. To make the first markings, create the basic grid to draw your log cabin using a flexible ruler. For help building the grid, see General Instructions.

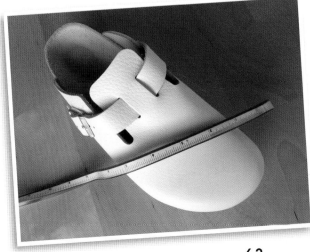

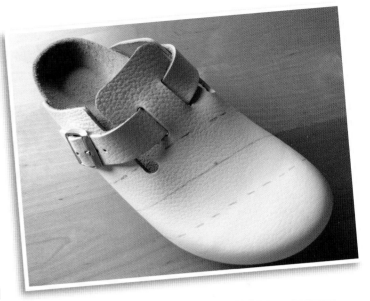

3a. The basic framework of squares is the most important element of the Log Cabin clog. Your squares should be as square as possible. On a curved surface that's about as hard as it gets. Do it step by step.

3b. The squares will be 1" x 1" and will be built up from your baseline. Keep the flexible ruler at a 90-degree angle on your baseline. Then make marks at 1" above your baseline and 1" under. Do this in several spots, so you create a dotted parallel line under and above the baseline.

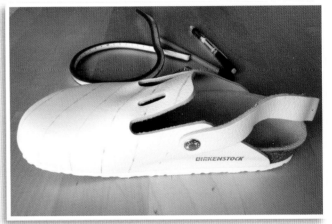

3c. Connect these dots through a line. Using your flexible ruler will help a lot! These 3 lines are your starting point to make parallel lines to the top and to the toe, each 1" apart. Sometimes you will have to push a little harder to get around the corners, especially at the toe. Working in dots and connecting them works best for me.

4. If all your diagonal lines are done, take the next step: draw the line from top to sole. The line goes through your focus point at a 90-degree angle from the top to the side of your shoe. Repeat the line 1" to each side, just like you did with the lines based on the baseline.

When you finish these 90-degree angle lines, you end up with a 1" square pattern on your clog.

On the toe you will have to deal with curved lines. Don't try to make a square inch on your toe. It will be very difficult to make your lines straight. Pretend your fabric pulls together on the toe.

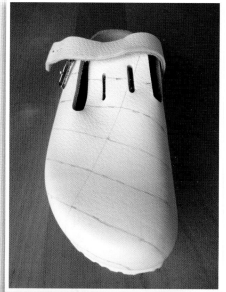

If you have a shoe with a strap on top, two issues arise: How to deal with the gaps (slits for the strap) on top; and how to deal with the strap itself. For the gaps I decided to make them part of the design, as if the gaps were made later. The lines continue, as that influences the grid the least.

Regarding the grid on the strap, first draw the lines on the body of the shoe. Then put in the strap and adjust it to the right hole. You can follow the grid of the body from the shoe on the strap. The grid on the strap will not be 1" x 1", as the strap is curving under and on top of the body of the shoe. Do not worry about that. That part of the grid is under the body of the shoe.

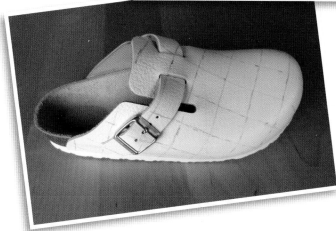

5a. Now that the grid is drawn, you can start making Log Cabins with pencils. The layout in this design is a basic Log Cabin, so every block has the same build up. If you decide to experiment with thunderbolts or other layouts, first make an example on paper. As soon as you put your lines on your shoe, you might start getting confused about what the position should be to or from the next block.

Start here and follow the arrows

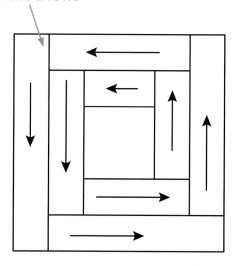

First shoe

5b. To draw a Log Cabin block, divide the square into 6ths. Start on the left at $1/6$ of your block (approximately $3/16$" in from the outside line) and draw a vertical line from the top to the bottom of your square. The next line follows at $1/6$ of your first line (approximately $3/16$"), and goes to the third side. At $1/6$ of your second line, you draw the third line to the fourth side (approximately $3/16$"). Each line follows the other, until you have created a log cabin with eight lines.

5c. The first block is the design of this pattern. If you decide to make a different build up of Log Cabin blocks, check how each block has to start. Make a

Log Cabins Afoot

decision up front and be sure to have a drawn layout available as a guide while you are drawing. This gives you the opportunity to check your progress. As soon as you have ten blocks in pencil on your shoe, the lines might look all the same to you! Stay focused.

6. Now that you have decided how your block layout will be, take your pencil and start drawing the lines on your shoe.

Don't be too fussy; start with your longest line at approximately $\frac{1}{6}$ ($\frac{3}{16}$") and just keep going.

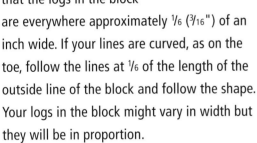

As you may have noticed, not every block is exactly the same, and especially around the strap, making your blocks can be difficult. Keep in mind that the logs in the block are everywhere approximately $\frac{1}{6}$ ($\frac{3}{16}$") of an inch wide. If your lines are curved, as on the toe, follow the lines at $\frac{1}{6}$ of the length of the outside line of the block and follow the shape. Your logs in the block might vary in width but they will be in proportion.

The lines on the strap follow the lines of the body of the shoe. That creates an ongoing design. When all lines are put on the shoe with pencil, you are ready for the next step.

7a. Grab your paint or markers and some paper to find out what your color combination will be. Usually I have a very simple try out, just putting the colors in combination with each other in a doodle.

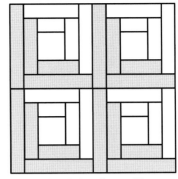
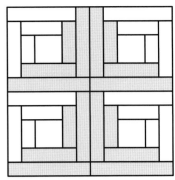

Single block pattern   **Triangle pattern**

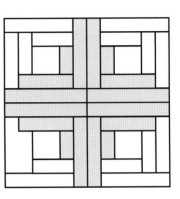

Quad block pattern

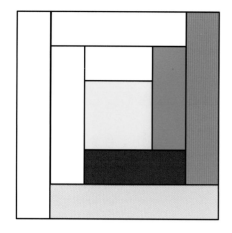

A log cabin is divided in two triangles, a dark triangle and a light triangle, each built out of four logs surrounding a square.

In this design, the light triangle of the log cabin is left white, to create an open design.

For the dark side I used blue, sky blue, navy, and lime to create a bright and consistent design. The yellow heart (center square) creates the sparkle.

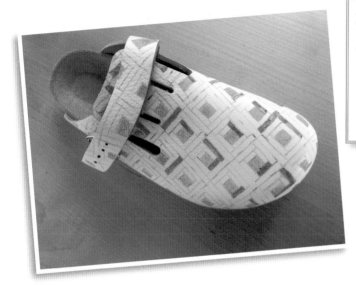

Note: *When you work with leather paint, you will have to paint the white side white. Preparation with acetone makes it necessary to paint the whole shoe. With markers or fabric paint, the white material of the shoe just shows through.*

7b. Start with the heart of the log cabin. All squares will be the same yellow. These centers will help you keep track of which logs to color what.

7c. Then begin with your lightest color, sky blue. Keep in mind which side of the block you want to color. A mistake is easily made!

7d. In general, 1 log per block is sky blue, as you have 4 colors and 4 logs to color. However, be creative and switch the logs you choose for the same color. Just keep coloring. After the sky blue, use the lime, then the blue, then the navy. If you are working with permanent markers, fine markers might be too bold for the tiny logs. You may choose to work with the ultrafine markers. If you are working with paint, the tiny logs might be helped with a tiny pencil or even a toothpick.

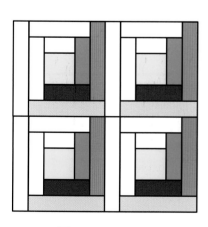

Standard log
color and position

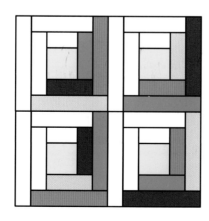

Variation in log
color and position

Log Cabins Afoot

7e. Switching position of the log color in your blocks makes the pattern more creative. Also, try to differ in the use of the colors in one block. Some blocks may have two sky blue logs, and miss a navy; some blocks may have two lime logs and no sky blue. Variation keeps your design interesting! Compare the group of blocks on page 67. Where the standard group might become a bit dull, the second asks you to keep looking. That's what you need when you are looking for just great shoes!

7f. When dealing with the strap, check the colors on the body of the shoe, and choose the same color for the strap to have it blend in with the body of the shoe. Your shoe is now colored, but your logs are hardly visible, as the pencil marks are very light and erasable. Above that, the shoe is lacking contrast. So you are ready for the final step.

8. For the fencing off (outlining) step you will need a steady hand. Be sure your shoe is as dry as possible. Then take your ultrafine black marker and start marking first the blocks. After all the blocks have been marked, mark the lines around the logs. You can follow the same system as how you put on the pencil markings—start at the upper left and just go counterclockwise.

After this step, your first shoe is finished!

9a. To get the same look on the second shoe, mark the second shoe's focal point the same way as you did with the first one. Then put the second shoe next to the first shoe, and make a pencil mark on the second shoe where the baseline on the inside of your first shoe starts.

Start here and follow the arrows

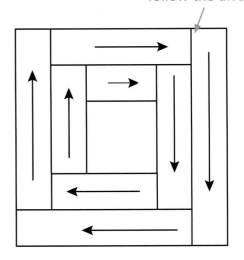

Second shoe

9b. Make your second shoe's baseline by connecting the focal point with this mark. Continue to set up your grid from your baseline.

9c. Be aware, drawing the logs on the second shoe will be mirrored. Your logs will be designed counterclockwise. Also, the coloring is mirrored. Not the bottom right, but the bottom left triangle is colored.

10. Finish the shoe according to the material (see General Instructions).

Patterns

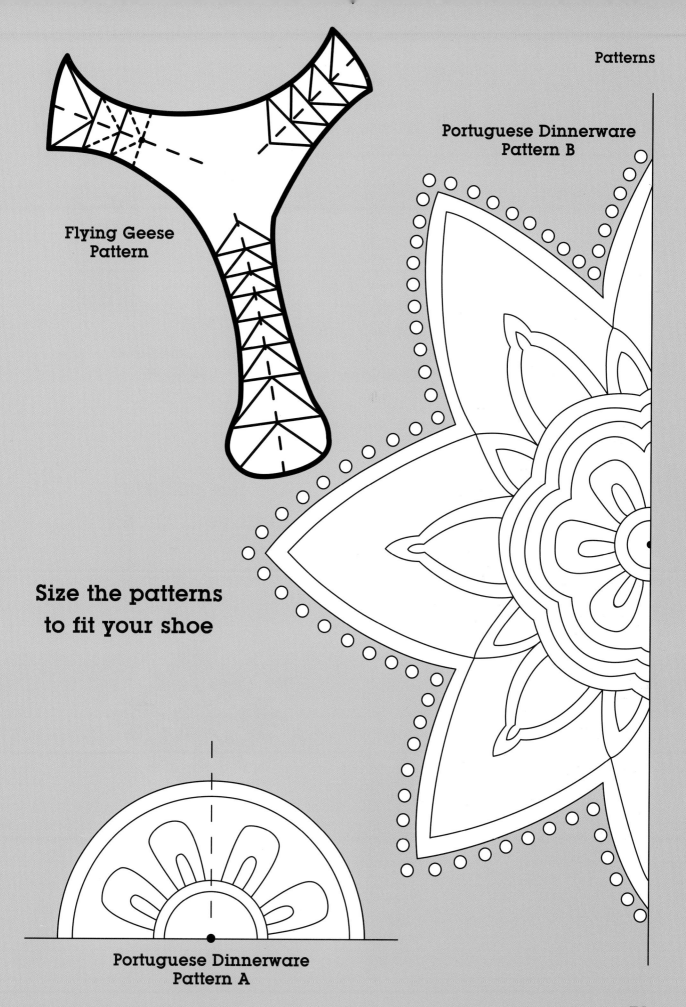

**Flying Geese
Pattern**

**Portuguese Dinnerware
Pattern B**

**Size the patterns
to fit your shoe**

**Portuguese Dinnerware
Pattern A**

**Mariner's Compass
(front of shoe)**

**Mariner's Compass
stars**

Size the patterns
to fit your shoe

**Mariner's Compass
Fleur-de-Lys
(side of shoe)**

**Hawaiian cutout
copyright by
©Pokelele**

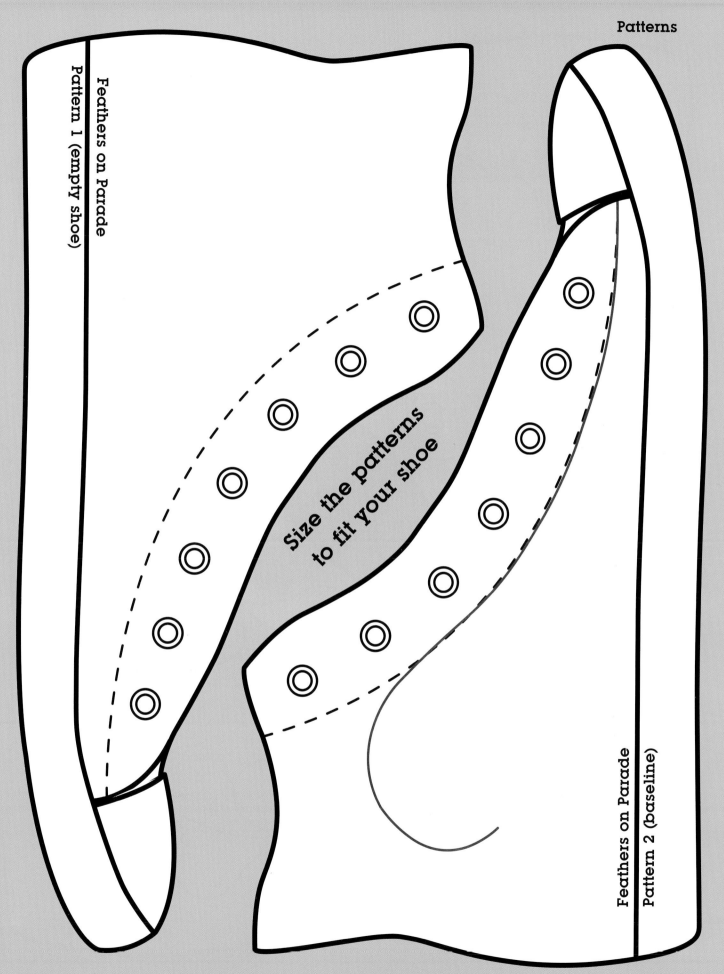

Feathers on Parade

Pattern 1 (empty shoe)

Size the patterns to fit your shoe

Feathers on Parade

Pattern 2 (baseline)

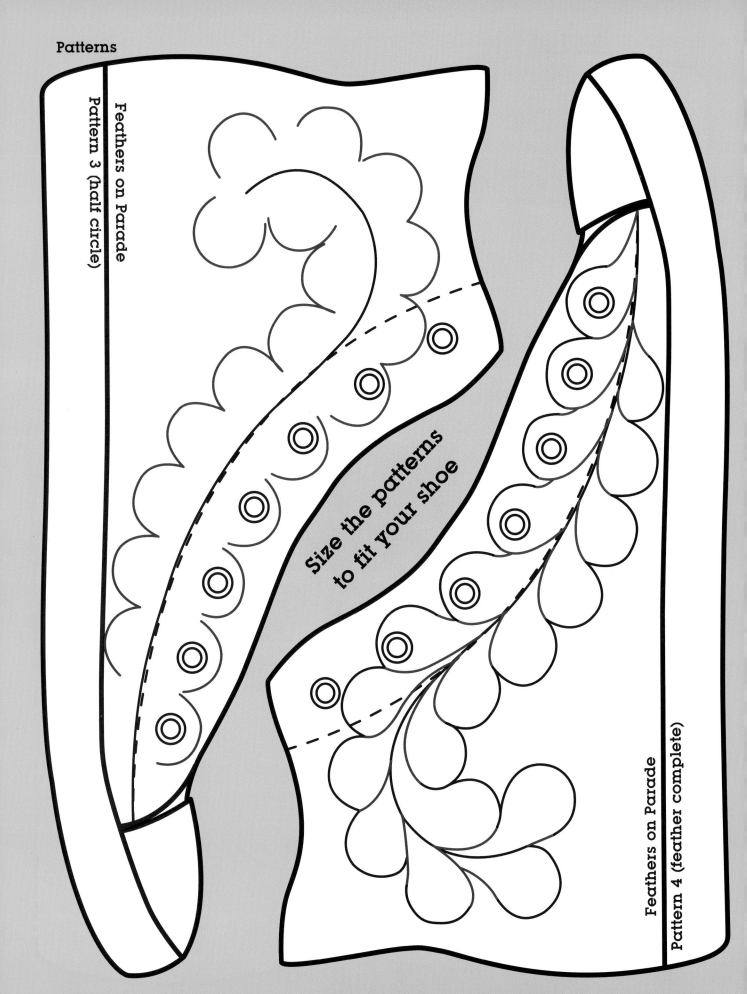

Feathers on Parade
Pattern 3 (half circle)

Size the patterns
to fit your shoe

Feathers on Parade
Pattern 4 (feather complete)

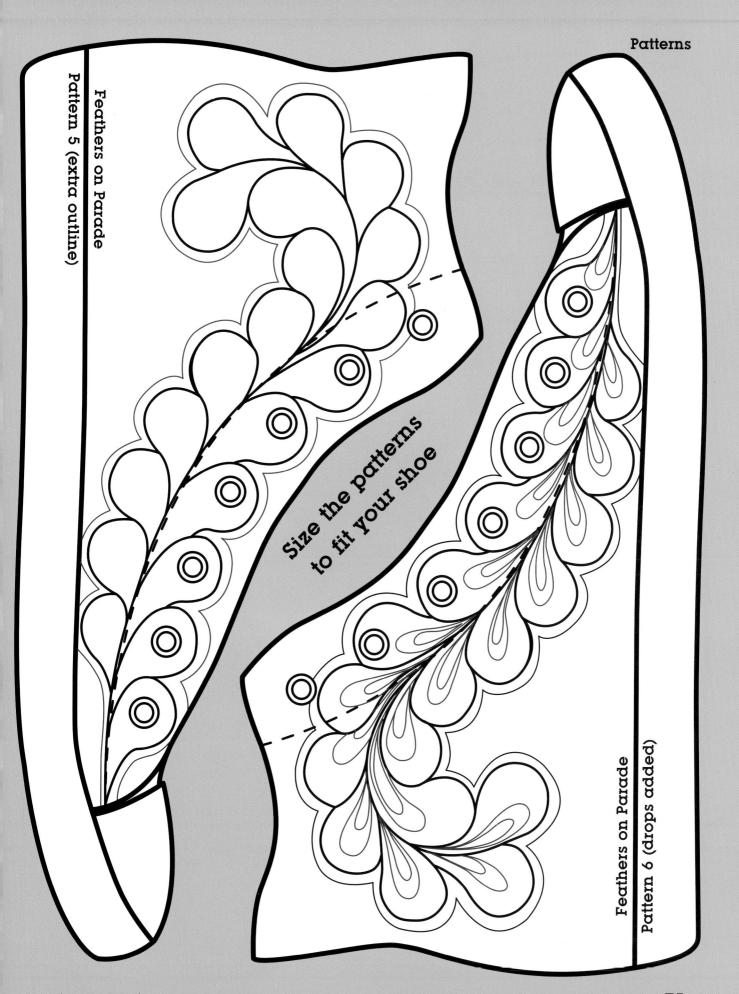

Feathers on Parade

Pattern 5 (extra outline)

Size the patterns to fit your shoe

Feathers on Parade

Pattern 6 (drops added)

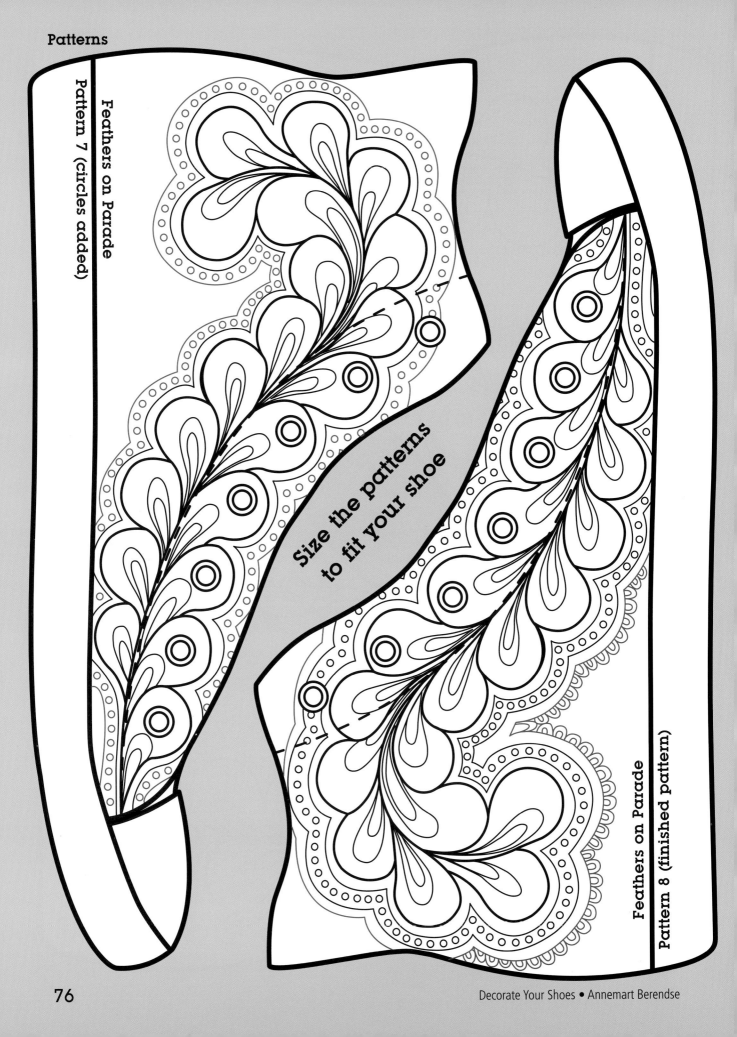

Feathers on Parade

Pattern 7 (circles added)

Size the patterns to fit your shoe

Feathers on Parade

Pattern 8 (finished pattern)

Decorate Your Shoes • Annemart Berendse

Size the patterns to fit your shoe

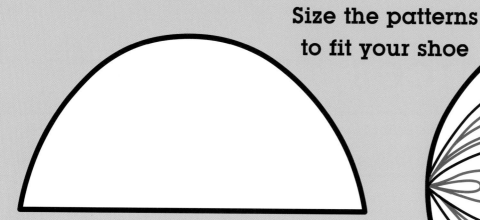

Feathers on Parade
Toe Pattern 1
(empty toe)

Feathers on Parade
Toe Pattern 4
(droplets in leaves)

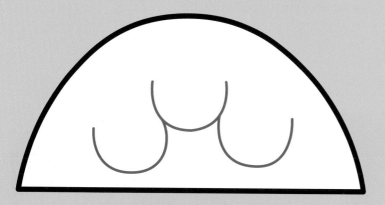

Feathers on Parade
Toe Pattern 2
(first marking)

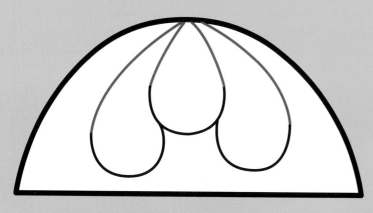

Feathers on Parade
Toe Pattern 3
(leaves drawn)

Feathers on Parade
Toe Pattern 5
(finished pattern)

Resources

- **Starter sets, paint, pencils, brushes, ruler, and a selection of markers**
  http://www.feetofcreativity.com/

- **Hexagon templates**
  http://www.paperpieces.com

- **Foam stickers**
  Toy store, craft shop for children

- **Chemicals such as alcohol, glue, and acetone**
  Local hardware store, big box, or other warehouse store

- **More information, pictures, video instructions, and contact with the author**
  www.quiltingthetownred.com or www.quiltingthetownred.com/tutorials

Meet the Author

Receiving a mother-in-law who had quilting as her hobby was the greatest marriage gift in disguise Annemart Berendse could get. Especially because quilters are not widespread in the Netherlands.

When, in 2001, her mother-in-law wanted to make a quilt for her, Annemart needed to select some quilt fabric in a local quilt shop. She ended up with not only the fabric for the quilt her mother-in-law would make, but also some fat quarters and no idea what to do with them. She was advised to start with a Nine Patch.

Never afraid to start something new without the hindrance of knowing what to do, she began sewing that same night. And as an Eight-pointed Star looked better to her, she decided to start with that pattern. The next morning, when the first quilt lesson with her mother-in-law began, the block was finished. Not made according to the rules of the quilt police, and it was a start of a passion for life. And that's how Annemart still works: Just try and be creative, and foremost, have fun! This first attempt resulted in a passion for living for quilting and everything related to it.

Born and living in the Netherlands where quilting is not as big as in the US, Annemart's focus went quickly to the states for inspiration, shows, and meeting American quilters. For her, quilting is her fountain of fun and creativity next to her full-time job as a department manager. Although she focuses on making all her points meet and getting 14 stitches to an inch, if there is no joy in making the quilt, for her, it's not a quilt.

This same joy she put into the design of her own quilting shoes when going to the 2011 AQS quilt show in Paducah. All the great reactions to that pair of shoes made her decide to develop more designs and write a book, the same way she learned how to quilt: Just jump in and try, be creative, and have fun!

Annemart is still married to the same spouse (and thus has the same mother-in-law) and lives in the Netherlands. She regularly comes over to the US to visit shows, to be inspired, to meet American quilters, and to enjoy the creativity of quiltmakers from all over the world. She hopes you have the same positive reactions while wearing your quilting "shoes for show" and have loads of fun making one-of-a-kind footwear.

Contact Annemart at http://www.quiltingthetownred.com.

More Books from AQS

This is only a small selection of the books available from the American Quilter's Society. AQS books are known worldwide for timely topics, clear writing, beautiful color photos, and accurate illustrations and patterns. The following books are available from your local bookseller, quilt shop, or public library.

#8349

#8664

#7610

#8532

#8025

#8665

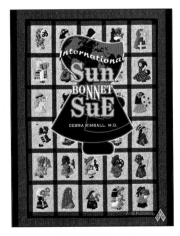

#8347

#8523

#8351